Gary David Comstock

The Work
of a Gay College Chaplain

*Pre-publication
REVIEWS,
COMMENTARIES,
EVALUATIONS . . .*

"This work is an astonishing combination of deeply moving professional memoir and highly creative practical pedagogy for any educator who wants to create a classroom community where authenticity, genuine inquiry, and inclusivity are possible. Regardless of which group he worked with—preschool children, students from prestigious colleges as well as community colleges, or prison inmates—Comstock brought a capacity to listen deeply to peoples' needs and provide the tools that empower them to become more fully human.

As a gay chaplain and professor, Comstock has indeed succeeded in not seeking 'a place at the table,' but changing 'the shape, color, size, and seating arrangement of the table.' He gives us a new understanding of how parents and teachers can meet the of-ten neglected and misunderstood needs of gay children. Chronicling his journey as a gay professional working primarily with straight people, he 'constructs a theoretical and practical model for relating to people whose experience is different than our own.' This model, and many of the pedagogical strategies he offers, provides universal understanding for a time when it is urgent that we learn to work constructively with our deepest differences.

I recommend this book to parents, professors, teachers at all grade levels, pedagogical theorists, policymakers, and anyone who strives to be a leader in today's organizations or communities. All of these readers will find stories that will touch their heart and wisdom that will change the way they work with young people and anyone who appears to be an 'other' in their life."

Rachael Kessler, MA
Director, The Institute for Social
and Emotional Learning;
Author, *The Soul of Education*

"**G**ary Comstock has done it again. As in *Gay Theology Without Apology*, he writes with a scholar's care, a pastor's compassion, and a man's feel for spiritual living across human differences. Few are those who combine so many talents to such brilliant and persuasive effect.

The Work of a Gay College Chaplain is a book for everyone. Any pastor who must attend to congregations of mixed, even harsh, differences of opinion will find Comstock to be a fountain of practical wisdom. Religious leaders who serve predominantly secular institutions such as most colleges and universities will learn how to keep and witness to one's faith quietly but with conviction. Those who enjoy the pleasures and on occasion suffer the abuses visited upon queers of all orientations will draw inspiration from this man. He has fought (and written about) all the battles, without sacrificing an iota of the dignity and pleasure of the queer life. In short, anyone, of whatever life or faith, who struggles with spiritual living among religion's cultured despisers will want to read this wonderful book again and again."

Charles Lemert, PhD
Professor of Sociology,
Wesleyan University,
Middletown, Connecticut

"**T**he Work of a Gay College Chaplain* is an intriguing book that follows the author on an intellectual, emotional, and spiritual journey. In it, Comstock explores both the many facets of himself and the process by which he has learned to serve others most fully as a counselor, a leader, and a teacher. This is an honest work that is based on the actual experiences of Comstock's life, together with the material he has studied to help him reach his current understanding. Comstock is a man of faith, and it is an inclusive, embracing faith that draws people close rather than excluding those who do not fit in.

The Work of a Gay College Chaplain begins with the questions concerning fathering gay children and working with three- and four-year-olds. The principles of acceptance of difference, of encouraging breadth of learning, of allowing each person one serves to be himself or herself as fully as possible are effectively explored.

As Comstock continues to take us on his journey into the college classroom, we find the same issues raised and highlighted in a new framework. This opened up for me the possibilities implicit within all of my life. How can I use the classrooms where I teach to enable my students to learn more deeply about who they are? How can I see within myself the depth of possibilities that I often overlook? As Comstock explores various anthropologists' perspectives on life, he opens for us the opportunity to look at our own lives as would an anthropologist: with interest in the most mundane details, with joy at uncovering new truths, with appreciation for our uniqueness. Comstock's work speaks to me as a rabbi, a lesbian, a teacher, and a parent. It can open for all of us new ways to approach our lives and the lives of our students, our children, and our friends, whether or not they are gay or lesbian."

Rabbi Linda Holtzman, MA
Director of Practical Rabbinics,
Reconstructionist Rabbinical College,
Wyncote, Pennsylvania

More pre-publication
REVIEWS, COMMENTARIES, EVALUATIONS . . .

"Like all of Gary David Comstock's work, this volume is a careful and thoughtful reflection on the lives of gays and lesbians that brings together information about everyday life with theoretical reflection informed by a range of social scientific and theological perspectives. And, like all of his work, *The Work of a Gay College Chaplain* emphasizes what it is that gays and lesbians bring to our world as visible, contributing citizens. Here, rather than interviews or statistical analyses, Comstock's efforts to build out from hope into justice draw on his own experience as a gay man weaving together theory and life; in this volume, he weaves together autobiography and theoretical reflection. As always, he reminds us not of the limitations or constraints of the gay or lesbian world, but of what that world—and we—contribute to making the world in which we live a better place. As always, his research is 'situated' with gay and lesbian people; here, Comstock draws on his own interior monologue and his own rich life to think hopefully forward."

Susan E. Henking, PhD
Associate Professor,
Religious Studies,
Hobart and William Smith Colleges,
Geneva, New York

Harrington Park Press®
An Imprint of The Haworth Press, Inc.
New York • London • Oxford

The Work
of a Gay College Chaplain
Becoming Ourselves
in the Company of Others

HARRINGTON PARK PRESS
Titles of Related Interest

The Work
of a Gay College Chaplain
Becoming Ourselves
in the Company of Others

Gary David Comstock

Harrington Park Press®
An Imprint of The Haworth Press, Inc.
New York • London • Oxford

Published by

Harrington Park Press®, an imprint of The Haworth Press, Inc., 10 Alice Street, Binghamton, NY 13904-1580

Selections from Thich Nhat Hanh, *Peace Is Every Step: The Path of Mindfulness in Everyday Life* (New York: Bantam Books, 1991) printed with permission from Random House, Inc. Excerpts (182 words) by Hermann Hesse, from SIDDHARTHA, copyright © 1951 by New Directions Publishing Corp. Reprinted by permission of New Directions Publishing Corp. Excerpts from James (Jimmy) E. Jones, "Why I Am a Muslim," in Edith S. Engel and Henry W. Engel, eds., *One God: Peoples of the Book* (Cleveland: The Pilgrim Press, 1990), reprinted with permission from The Pilgrim Press. Excerpts totaling 1033 words from WITH A DAUGHTER'S EYE by MARY CATHERINE BATESON. COPYRIGHT © 1984 BY MARY CATHERINE BATESON. Reprinted by permission of HarperCollins Publishers, Inc. WILLIAM MORROW. Excerpts from Susan Isaacs, *Intellectual Growth in Young Children* (London: Routledge & Kegan Paul Ltd, 1930; sixth impression, 1950) printed with permission from Routledge, member of the Taylor & Francis Group, United Kingdom. Excerpts from "Ceremony," copyright © 1977 by Leslie Marmon Silko, reprinted with permission of The Wylie Agency. Excerpts from pp. 89, 105 totaling 138 words, from THE SPIRAL DANCE; A REBIRTH OF THE ANCIENT RELIGION OF THE GODDESS. DELUXE, TENTH ANNIVERSARY EDITION by STARHAWK. Copyright © 1979, 1989 by Miriam Simos. Reprinted by permission of HarperCollins Publishers, Inc.

Cover design by Marylouise E. Doyle.

Library of Congress Cataloging-in-Publication Data

Comstock, Gary David, 1945-
    The work of a gay college chaplain : becoming ourselves in the company of others / Gary David Comstock.
        p. cm.
    Inclues bibliographical references and index.
    ISBN 1-56023-360-5 (alk. paper) — ISBN 1-56023-361-3 (pbk. : alk. paper)
    1. Homosexuality—Religious aspects—Christianity. 2. Gays—Religious life. I. Title.
BR115.H6 C674 2001
261.8'35766—dc21
                                                                                00-047215

Dedicated to Ted, in whose presence
and love I have become myself.

ABOUT THE AUTHOR

Gary David Comstock, PhD, is the University Protestant Chaplain and Associate Professor of Sociology at Wesleyan University, Middletown, Connecticut. He earned his PhD from Union Theological Seminary. The Reverend Dr. Comstock is the co-editor of *Que(e)rying Religion: A Critical Anthology* (1997) and the author of *A Whosoever Church: Welcoming Lesbians and Gay Men into African-American Congregations* (2000); *Unrepentant, Self-Affirming, Practicing: Lesbian/Bisexual/Gay People Within Organized Religion* (1996); *Gay Theology Without Apology* (1993); and *Violence Against Lesbians and Gay Men* (1991). He is an ordained clergyperson within the United Church of Christ.

CONTENTS

Preface

BEGINNING

In 1963, when I moved away from home to become a college freshman, I could not have imagined that one day I would live openly as a gay man. In high school I had accepted and lived with the separation of my feelings from my social life. Having secret fantasies about men, but dating and behaving as a normal heterosexual, was the "arrangement" I made with myself as my desires peaked in conflict with social norms and expectations. During my first months as a college freshman, however, such an arrangement became unbearable. My attraction to men seemed to increase and be at unresolvable odds with preparing for a lifelong profession. I was convinced that my feelings—acted on or not—would distract me from and most likely destroy a productive professional life. In place of my previous "arrangement," I made and enforced a more hard-and-fast "deal": I would not even allow myself to have secret yearnings and fantasies. As I accepted and took on each layer of what was socially expected, I socially "agreed" to let myself dim and fade. During the next four years of college, I became a serious art major and relied heavily on alcohol to get me through a blurry and rowdy pattern of dating and partying.

After college, I fumbled through two years of graduate study in art history with little direction and near panic. I was afraid and ignorant of what I really wanted to do. At times, ending my life seemed to make more sense than continuing it. But the Stonewall riots were a pivotal historical event that changed my life. In 1969, when I had just finished my second year of graduate school, the patrons of a gay bar in New York's Greenwich Village resisted the customary efforts of police officers to harass, intimidate, and arrest them. Their resistance extended into several days of street violence with the police that marked the beginning of the Gay Liberation Movement of the 1970s.

Hearing about homosexuals who openly and collectively defied the authorities brought me out of self-pity and self-defeat. Although I was not certain which profession, if any, I would ever become a part of, I learned that neighborhoods of gay men did exist and that I could live in them. I left the East Coast for Seattle and San Francisco. Without making a conscious decision to do so, I stopped drinking the day I visited my first gay bar. Although the gay scene consisted almost exclusively of bar life, alcohol was suddenly of no interest to me. For the next four years I lived openly as a gay man and supported myself with a variety of low-paying jobs. I gave little thought to what I would do in the future, and instead I simply "danced my heart out" in a social and cultural scene in which I felt accepted and relaxed.

BECOMING

I now think of this period as the adolescence that I should have had in high school and college. And as happens with adolescence, especially when one can express and fulfill one's feelings, I eventually tired of it and was ready to move on. I got a job teaching art in a high school and saved my money so I could head back to graduate school. This move was both a return and a new start. I returned to the East Coast and to the academic life, but to study in two areas in which I had taken no courses in college—religion and sociology. I also reconnected with my biological family and with the religious denomination of my youth, but under different conditions—ones that allowed me to become myself. I was not seeking their permission or acceptance. I had decided that I would be openly gay and they would get used to and like it.

My return was not a dramatic barnstorming confrontation. I did not shout and scream, nor did they. I simply insisted on doing everything without hiding that I was gay. I applied to graduate school, earned my degrees, was ordained, and became a chaplain and professor as an openly gay man. I brought my lover to family gatherings, and we subsequently got invited to them. I did most things with the assumption that I not only belonged but that I could and should make a difference. I was not seeking "a place at the table," because I knew there were things wrong with "the table" that I had fled from years earlier. I did not want to fit in as much as I wanted to change the shape, color, size, and seating arrangement of the table. Some of those changes were more difficult to achieve than others. My ordination, for example, was blocked four times, but my belated adolescence in the gay ghetto of San Francisco had provided me with the pride and confidence with which to endure and persist. I was ready to live all aspects of my life—personal, religious, professional—as an openly gay man, and society, too, was becoming somewhat more ready for lesbians and gay men to make our contributions.

This book is about my professional interactions with nongay people—relationships that I could not have begun to imagine when I was a college student and that I have been able to create as one person among the growing number of openly gay professionals. As few as we may be, we see ourselves not as hidden and despised but as visible and contributing members of society. Whereas most gay people once saw themselves as abnormal and in need of help, now as openly gay doctors, clergy, public officials, lawyers, social workers, therapists, and teachers, we are providing and administering help to nongay people.[1]

I do not wish to invert the social order by saying that nongay people need all the help they can get and gay people are the most qualified to give it. Rather, I am saying that gradually gay people have been taking their place among the ranks of professionals to make their own contributions. Sometimes our contributions maintain the status quo, and sometimes they challenge and change it. I am more interested in how openly gay people are making changes and helping people in new ways.

WORKING

The following chapters are about my becoming the openly gay college chaplain and professor I am today. Chapter 1, "Fathering Gay Children," reaches back into my childhood to a fundamental resource—my relationship with my father. Even though gay people often recall their childhoods as difficult or even dangerous, I find that I rely upon much of what my father did when I reach out to others. His relationship with me provides the major theme of the book—listening to others and learning from them what they need, rather than telling and imposing on them what one thinks they should do. In this chapter, those who are listened to and learned from are "effeminate" boys, including myself, but not before I examine how and why the current psychiatric profession, gay community, queer theory, and men's movement continue to disapprove of, avoid, or reject these young people. I attempt to show that by listening to them we hear the words that rescue other kids, that provide answers to what they need and want, that inform and change how we relate to young people in general and to one another.

Chapter 2, "Learning from and with Children," is my attempt to develop a preschool curriculum that counters our tendency to impose on children adult ways of being in the world. Instead of doing something to or for them so they will be like us or like what we would like them to be, I look for ways to help children discover and create themselves. I review theories and practices of early childhood education from the past two hundred years, and then, drawing from my experience as a head teacher at Union Seminary's Day Care Center when I was a graduate student, I offer and discuss suggestions for learning from and with young children.

In Chapter 3, "Examining Preconceptions," I turn to my first and subsequent college teaching jobs. Instead of a teaching style whereby the teacher deposits information and the student accepts the teacher's knowledge, I try to help students identify their own problems and produce their own knowledge. I discuss my development of what Paulo Freire calls a dialogical, rather than monological, approach in the three different settings in which I have taught—a nonselective Roman Catholic professional college, a maximum security correctional facility, and a highly selective liberal arts university.[2] Recognizing, expressing, and working with "unacceptable" feelings—such as racism, homophobia, sexism, and other forms of hatred or anger—is one of the issues I examine.

In Chapter 4, "Interfacing," I construct a theoretical and practical model for relating to people whose experience is different from our own. My resources are lesbian-of-color writers who warn against ranking oppressions, Margaret Mead's cross-cultural anthropology, and Donna Haraway's theory of "situated knowledges." I apply my model to my work with adolescent and young adult men, a social group with whom I interact daily, and also the social group statistically most likely to engage in antigay violence and to harbor homophobic feelings.

Chapter 5, "Writing for Students," applies further the interface model from the previous chapter as I discuss writing about topics of interest to students in a way that is accessible to them. At my liberal arts residential university, such writing includes prayers for large events, letters and articles for the student newspaper, and talks and speeches at student-organized events. I also try to understand and write about academic topics from the viewpoint of students. An example I provide is my discussion of biblical authorship, in which I use the language and experience of a female college student.

In Chapter 6, "Creating Worship," I describe how I have developed a weekly service that brings together Jews, Catholics, Protestants, Buddhists, Hindus, Muslims, agnostics, and atheists. The service provides an informal time for people to relax, discuss spirituality, create ritual, and share dinner in a comfortable setting. My most challenging and satisfying work as a chaplain has been to find a way for people to express, question, and share their beliefs and interests with one another and to find greater meaning in their lives with and among those who are not like them. This kind of service challenges conventional ways of imaging God and defining worship. I rely on the German Resistance theologian Dietrich Bonhoeffer to help me to image God as mutuality-in-relationship and to define and practice worship as building mutual relationships with others. This image and these relationships provide for a new kind of leadership role for clergy that requires us to be "set among" and not "set apart."

Gary David Comstock

Chapter 1

Fathering Gay Children

A LACK OF RESOURCES

We do not have positive terms, let alone helpful resources, for discussing boys who do not conform to gender stereotypes, so we rely on "effeminate boys" with all its negative connotations. We are so familiar with our disapproval, avoidance, and rejection of these young people that to consider accepting them, taking them seriously, and learning from them jolts us from what we assume to be a time-honored and correct practice of silence and exclusion. A rare exception is Tomie de Paola's 1979 children's book *Oliver Button Is a Sissy*. In it, one reads that Oliver does not like to do what boys are supposed to do. Instead, he likes to jump rope, read, draw, dress up, sing, dance, and pretend to be a movie star. When his father disapproves and makes him go outside to play baseball, he is not picked for a team because he is not athletic. In response to his unhappiness and his preference for dancing, his parents relent and send him to dancing school. He learns quickly and practices a lot, but the boys tease him about his dancing shoes and write on the school wall: "OLIVER BUTTON IS A SISSY." His dance teacher enters him in a local talent show, his schoolteacher encourages his classmates to attend, and the audience enthusiastically applauds his performance. Oliver is disappointed because he does not win first prize, but his parents are very proud of him and take him out for pizza. When he goes to school the next day, he finds the earlier graffiti has been changed to "OLIVER BUTTON IS A STAR!"[1]

The author captures a familiar set of experiences for effeminate boys: disapproval, rejection, verbal abuse, and physical intimidation by parents and peers. However, the shift in this story to recognizing, encouraging, and applauding the wishes, talents, and activities of an effeminate boy is so exceptional as to stand as a model for what could and should be. But de Paola's book, too, makes compromises and conforms to gender norms. Oliver's outfit for the talent show is a conventionally male suit-and-tie, straw-hat, dancing-cane ensemble; and the first-place winner is a girl who twirls a baton and wears tasseled boots, a tiara, and a fringed, spangled leotard.

A foreign-language film, *Ma Vie en Rose* (My Life in Pink), released in the United States in 1998, portrays a family whose seven-year-old son does not hide his effeminacy.[2] The difficulties within the family are presented with unflinching honesty and reality, as are the reactions of those outside the family. The creativity, innocence, and beauty of the boy's wishes are juxtaposed with his realization that going to sleep in the freezer is the best way to end the problems his public cross-dressing has caused for his family. His parents' subsequent attempt to accept him "as is" results in the boy's removal from school by petition of other parents, the father's loss of employment, and the family's moving to another town because of shunning by neighbors. The one positive response—a teacher's talk with the boy's class about respecting differences—stands out for its inability to change the prevailing rejection, and the family's end-of-film situation—in a less affluent neighborhood and with a lower-paying job for the father—leaves the viewer with the harsh realities of, rather than practical suggestions for, parenting effeminate boys. However, the family's final decision to risk social rejection and to accept rather than change the boy is a rare and welcome model, even if it is more likely to happen in film than in life.

Without meaning to discredit either the book or the film, their limits as resources should be noted. De Paola's book has remained in print for twenty years but has not become a children's classic; and the impact that a foreign-language film will make on the American public is not great. Although critically acclaimed and an award winner at several film festivals, the low-budget, subtitled *Ma Vie en Rose* is not likely to capture the attention of American moviegoers. What follows is my own attempt to provide another resource—an example and model from my own childhood experience—to break the silence, to change the prevailing practice, to validate effeminate boys. But first I shall discuss in more depth the need for such a resource.

INVENTING AND PREVENTING TROUBLE

In her pioneering work in queer studies, Eve Kosofsky Sedgwick introduces and uses the term "proto-gay kids" to describe effeminate boys who become adult gay men.[3] As she points out, not all adult gay men have a childhood history of self-perceived effeminacy, but many studies have shown that gender nonconformity during childhood is more often associated with adult homosexuality than any other variable.[4] With the exception of Sedgwick's work, I know of no other professional literature that attempts to discuss boyhood effeminacy in positive terms. There is an interest in the dignified treatment of gay adults, but when it comes to children there is an aversion to, uneasiness about, or interest in reducing or correcting queer traits, effeminacy, and gender nonconformity.[5] Although the psychiatric profession did remove homosexuality from the 1980 edition of the *Diagnostic and Statistical Manual of Mental Disorders,* DSM-III, it inserted a new diagnosis: "302.60 Gender Identity Disorder of Childhood."[6] (Material quoted is reprinted with permission from the *Diagnostic and Statistical Manual of Mental Disorders,* Third Edition. Copyright 1980 American Psychiatric Association.)

The description in the DSM-III for this "disorder" includes both girls and boys, but gives more attention to boys. It is rife with inconsistencies and confusion. Despite claiming that this disorder "is not merely the rejection of stereotypical sex role behavior," but "a persistent repudiation of the individual's own anatomic attributes," the discussion focuses on conforming to stereotypes. That society (or the mental health profession) rather than the individual child is disturbed or disordered becomes ironically apparent when the description goes on to claim that for boys "gestures and actions are often judged against a standard of cultural stereotype to be feminine, and the boy is invariably subjected to male peer group teasing and rejection, which rarely occurs among girls until adolescence." The social response to these children would suggest that the conflict or problem lies within society's perception of these children rather than the children's self-perception. That the mental health profession invents this "disorder" and imposes it on children is revealed by its own conclusion that "most children with this disorder deny being disturbed by it except as it brings them into conflict with the expectations of their family or peers." The DSM-IV of 1994 focuses even more on the child's "persistent discomfort" with "cultural expectations" rather than with their own desires and preferences. Would not such children be better served by a profession that turned instead to those who disturb them and sought to label and treat the "disorder" of familial and social expectations that damage their development and happiness?[7]

The organized lesbian/gay community itself has not helped much in attending to and normalizing the feelings and experiences of proto-gay kids. Seeking entrance to mainstream politics and fearing empirically unfounded, politically motivated allegations that lesbians and gay men recruit children, the gay political movement has avoided the concerns of this population.[8] Some social services and school programs have been developed for gay adolescents, but not for preteens.[9] Such avoidance and reluctance by older lesbians and gay men is based on real and not imagined consequences.[10]

Sedgwick accurately observes that "teachers in the primary and secondary levels of public school . . . are subject to being fired . . . for providing any intimation that homosexual desires, identities, cultures, adults, children, or adolescents have a right to expression or existence."[11] And politicians have often stirred up opposition to efforts by school boards and administrators to introduce children's books about gay parents.[12] Perhaps the most spectacular example was the dismissal in 1993 of Joseph Fernandez, chancellor of the New York City public school system, for his attempt to implement the "Children of the Rainbow" curriculum.[13]

Under attack in the 443 page guide for this curriculum was a brief section for first-graders titled "Families," in which teachers were told to "be aware of varied family structures, including two-parent or single-parent households, gay or lesbian parents, divorced parents, adoptive parents, and guardians or foster parents."[14] Although other sections of the curriculum guide offered lessons, there were none here and no recommendations to discuss sex, sexuality, or homosexuaity. Teachers were simply urged to encourage tolerance of different families, including those headed by lesbians and gay men. Also attacked were two children's' books, *Heather Has Two Mommies* by Leslea Newman and *Daddy's Roommate* by Michael Willhoite, listed among the curriculum's 600 recommended but not required readings.[15] Since these efforts sought to introduce tolerance for the adult gay community, one can easily imagine that the response and consequences would be much harsher for programs seeking to recognize and validate proto-gay kids themselves.

In addition to gay politicians and community leaders, gay intellectuals, too, as represented by the dominant school of constructionist theory, shy away from recognizing proto-gay kids, but for different reasons. Rejecting the "essentialist" or biological approach and its claim that one is born gay, a constructionist sees gayness as a socially constructed or culturally constructed category and says, "I label myself (or society labels me) as gay." Essentialists also often assume that the term "gay" is universal and can be applied across historical periods and cultures, whereas constructionists argue that the particular terms for and understandings of same-sex oriented people within each period and culture should be discovered and recognized. For many constructionists, to recognize prepubescent gay identity and experience is to acknowledge an inherent, biological, or natural quality that is brought to and shapes adolescent sexuality. Such essential or natural contributions to sexual development are dismissed in favor of the sociocultural formation of sexual identities.[16]

However, less rigid constructionists do not see sexual identity and development in such either/or terms. Sedgwick, herself a leading constructionist scholar, credits essentialists for "recognizing and validating the creativity and heroism of the effeminate boy or tommish girl of the fifties (or sixties or seventies or eighties)."[17] And another leading constructionist theorist, Judith Butler, does turn to her own childhood and recalls the experiences that give insight into why proto-gay kids are "troubled":

> To make trouble was, within the reigning discourse of my childhood, something one should never do precisely because that would get one in trouble. The rebellion and the reprimand seemed to be caught up in the same terms, a phenomenon that gave rise to my first critical insight into the subtle ruse of power: The prevailing law threatened one with trouble, all to keep one out of trouble.[18]

Butler names and defines the "prevailing law" as official troublemaking predicated on and prohibiting personal troublemaking; in other words, "threatening one with trouble . . . to keep one out of trouble".[19]

The enforcement in public policy of what Butler calls the "prevailing law" is illustrated in two cases separated by a decade. In 1989 the U.S. Department of Health and Human Services repudiated its own study and findings that gay youth are two to three times more likely than other young people to attempt or commit suicide. This finding was deleted from its final report on youth not because of any alleged inaccuracy, but because, in the words of Secretary Louis Sullivan, it does not "represent my personal beliefs or the policy of this Department."[20] Sullivan effectively enforced his own trouble or the trouble he represented—"the prevailing law"—by denying the real trouble that kids are in and by preventing its being taken seriously.

The making of trouble for proto-gay kids in the form of institutionalized physical violence and psychological abuse was revealed in 1999 in a Federal class-action lawsuit brought against New York City by six children in its foster care system. The plaintiffs reported constant harassment, broken bones, and rape by peers, foster parents, and staff members. For example, staff members at group homes and treatment facilities rarely intervened when other children targeted a nine-year-old boy because he was effeminate. His nose was broken twice, his shoulder blade was broken, he was hit in the face with a broom, and he was thrown down a flight of stairs. The children claimed that their appeals for protection had been met with indifference, blame, and isolation. When one boy complained that his foster parents repeatedly humiliated him because of his feminine demeanor, an agency supervisor threatened to place him in a facility where tough boys would beat him up. The lawsuit cites an internal memo in which child welfare officials acknowledge that gay kids are "nearly impossible" to place because foster care agencies reject them or report that they are "scapegoated" by other children and staff members.[21]

This brief look at the mental health profession, the gay community, public education, and public policy unveils what seems to be a universal wish that proto-gay kids not exist or that they get over whatever it is that is bothering them without bothering us. As a society, we would prefer not to let the physical and psychological abuse that they suffer trouble us.

SOURCES OF INFORMATION FOR UNDERSTANDING THE NEEDS OF PROTO-GAY KIDS: HALTING VOICES

I turn my attention to proto-gay kids, particularly to effeminate boys, with a degree of retrospective self-interest and with a sense of humanitarian rescue. I have some scars from having hidden my own effeminacy as a child and from having been teased for what I could not hide; I want to protect today's effeminate boys from similar and worse scarring. But more importantly, I turn to them for answers, to rescue us, to reveal an avoided view of society that should inform and change us. To use the historian Donna Haraway's terms, I seek "the 'activation' of previously passive categories of objects of knowledge." I seek to surface their "limited voice for the sake of the connections and unexpected openings situated knowledges make possible."[22] "Situated knowledges" are what people know and learn from experiences within their particular social situations. Haraway points out that the socially powerful are more likely to ignore than to take seriously and learn from those whose situated knowledges threaten to change the status quo, and Secretary Sullivan's response to the study of youth suicides bears her out. What the subjugated and ignored know has the potential to spark inquiry that may unsettle preconceptions and familiar approaches. The particular "previously passive category of knowledge" that I seek to "activate" is the progressive, positive, and helpful fathering of proto-gay kids, because such fathering has been rare and therefore promises to open what is unexpected, least known, most avoided.

Much has been written and said by gay men about the problems we have experienced with our families of origin.[23] Many of us have learned to live openly outside of them because of an emerging and supportive lesbian/gay community. From a position of communal strength and autonomy, many of us no longer seek permission from our families of origin to be gay, but rather inform and interact with them on our own terms. And instead of dismissing our childhoods as hopeless pasts, against and in spite of which we became gay, we can now reconsider them with these questions: "What did we need as children to help us become gay adults?" and "Who and what helped us to become gay?"

Openly gay older men in the church and academy—such as myself—have the advantage of being able to listen and talk to our younger gay students, for whom relationships with fathers are not so much memories as living situations. Although these young people are no longer proto-gay kids, they provide a first step in linking us to them. What gay young men need from their fathers is captured in this fantasized visit from one student's father:

He meets me at my dorm room, and wants to come in. He knows how much my room means to me, and he is anxious for me to show it to him, since anything that is important to me is important to him. We walk in, and right away, he sees my over-sized poster of two men, one with his tongue in the other's ear. I show him my vanity table, replete with white doily, mod candle-sticks, hairspray and powder. He sees the framed picture of Ste-phen out on display, and comments on how attractive he is.

I then expose him to my shrine: my closet. First, he sees my blonde, Madonna-Who's-That-Girl wig, and asks if I've ever worn it. When I show him pictures of the last party to which I wore it, he laughs at my outlandish outfit. He then examines my display of necklaces and thumbs through the hanging items: a hot-pink plastic transparent vest; a cream-colored corset; a T-shirt with a picture on it of two men fucking. His eyes shift to my huge leopard-print hat, my chained leather cap, my gold glittery cowboy hat.

We go out to dinner, and later that night he comes to see me as Lady Enid in my favorite play, *The Mystery of Irma Vep.* He's proud of his son — his son the actor, the student, the lover, the occasional cross-dresser, the faggot.[24]

The facts for this young man are quite different from the fantasy. He also writes:

When I came out to my parents two years ago, they told me not to tell anyone. They particularly insisted that I not tell any-one in the family outside of my sisters. They told me never to tell them about my developments as a gay man, in terms of poli-tics, relationships, or social involvements. They told me that, by making the choice to come out, I have excluded them from my personal life. My life is no longer any of their business.[25]

When writing about their fathers, gay students express primarily the need for "love, acceptance, and support."[26] These terms may seem too general and sentimental to provide the basis for a detailed and pragmatic program for changing father-son relationships, but the fre-quency and consistency with which these needs are expressed should signal to us the seriousness with which we should take them.

CHANGING MEN?

Although a recognizable "men's movement" has emerged in the past three decades, it has focused on initiation, ritual, myth, and mass gatherings rather than on tending to affective needs and interpersonal relationships. As represented by the mythopoetical gatherings and best-selling books of Robert Bly, the Million Man March organized by the Nation of Islam, and the large stadium assemblies of the evangelical Christian organization, the Promise Keepers,[27] this movement has tried to reassert the role of the man-as-provider by recovering the lost rites of passage to manhood. Other less well-known but notable work does question and seek to develop alternatives to conventional notions of masculinity, but none of these focuses on and explores in depth fathering and father-son relationships.[28] Some scholars have observed a changing role for fathers in American society, but sociological studies show that "the man-as-breadwinner model of fatherhood. . . remains dominant today" and that a newer model of a nurturing father who is more engaged, accessible, and responsible for child care occupies a place in the middle-class *"culture of fatherhood* (specifically the shared norms, values, and beliefs surrounding men's parenting)," but not in "the *conduct of fatherhood* (what fathers do, their parental behaviors)."[29]

Sociologist Michael Messner summarizes the prevailing argument for emphasizing initiation, ritual, myth, and mass gatherings rather than attending to affective needs and interpersonal relationships as follows: Because "modern societies lack the masculine initiation rituals which so often characterized tribal societies, . . . today's men are confused about what it means to be a man" and the revival of such initiation rites and ancient myths "make men feel more secure about who they are." He also criticizes this argument as appealing to "middle-aged, white and professional-class men" and resting "on an overgeneralized and romanticized view of traditional tribal cultures."[30] But initiations have long been and still are a standard feature of fraternal organizations, sports teams, and the military, and they appeal to a wider class of men, as shown by the fascination of street gangs with initiation rituals.[31] Also, the Promise Keepers do not appropriate rites and myths associated with tribal cultures but with "the Pauline tradition of male leadership," "athletic and military metaphors of Christian spirituality," and "the 'Muscular Christian' movements of the late nineteenth and early twentieth centuries."[32] And some leaders of the mythopoetic wing of the men's movement claim they want to reform tribal initiatory practices as a way to alter, not to revive, a patriarchal model of manhood. They are not interested in re-establishing the role of man-as-provider; instead, they seek "to heal the wounds suffered by men" trying to live up to that role. Stephen Boyd, for example, claims that many men yearn for ritual spaces in which there is enough safety to explore and express their neglected emotions.[33] When the leader of one weekend retreat was asked, "How can we initiate our sons?" he responded, "We can't, because most of us have not been initiated. Maybe the best we can do is help each other initiate ourselves and then turn to the younger generation."[34] I would suggest, however, that instead of waiting until they "get it right" that they simply work, play, talk, and learn *with* their sons now.

The emphases on dramatic change through initiation and ritual, on recovering the role of provider and mentor, and on reclaiming or redefining masculine responsibilities that characterize the various manifestations of the men's movement are of little interest and relevance to most young gay men. The meaningful experiences that young gay men had wanted and needed with their fathers have little to do with instruction, initiation, and rites of passage to manhood. Young gay men were not looking for their fathers to initiate them into a previously held, traditional, or ideal version of manhood. They simply wanted their company, approval, and acceptance—the steady presence of and recognition by those who were most immediate to them.

However, Robert Bly does also emphasize that fathers and sons should spend "long hours together,"[35] (i.e., not setting aside "quality" time to do special things, but simply being together doing everyday activities such as chores, TV, and shopping.) And I think this kind of experience is meaningful and necessary for proto-gay kids. Within these kinds of activities a process of informal talking, listening, and familiarity can take place. But, I take issue with Bly's expectation and contention that in these hours together the son *receives* and the father *gives,* because I see the value of this informal, unstructured, nonspecialized time as a process in which the father does not feel obligated to press an agenda and is more likely to listen to his son and in which the son is more likely to feel encouraged to talk. Bly's concern for preserving and restoring the mentoring and initiating role of fathers—the one-way giving and instructional role—is one that I want to deflate. I do not trust fathers to perform that role and to recognize the needs of proto-gay kids, not because fathers are "bad" or inept people, but because they have been socialized to ignore and silence those needs.

PROBLEMS WITH INITIATION AND INSTRUCTION

What is wrong with initiation and instruction? One problem is that the initiator or instructor holds the power and authority. The initiate or student must submit to the requests or demands placed on him. Even in the seemingly benign and socially approved rites of passage that various religious bodies have created for marking the transition into adolescence, young people do not often feel engaged with or equal to those initiating them. Confirmations and Bar/Bat Mitzvahs are meant to provide long-term ties between the young person and his or her religious body, but, as Barry Kosmin and Seymour Lachman found in their 1993 study, *One Nation Under God,* "such rites of passage are of debatable value, since polarization seems to occur among adolescents immediately afterward; most feel they have 'graduated' and disappear from the life of the congregation."[36] Experts in the study of adolescence know the best "medium of growth in adolescence" are activities in which a teenager is "fully involved with challenging actions that test the limits of one's skills." Most important, teenagers need to have a say in what those activities should be and some control in planning them.[37] How many remember having to endure the preparation for Confirmation or Bar Mitzvah simply for the sake of their parents? Young people are often anxious about participating in these events, resentful of having to learn material that is not made relevant to their own experience, and relieved when the event is over.

To get a better understanding of problems that masculine initiation rituals pose for raising proto-gay kids, a broader view of initiations may be helpful. An African man told the writer Alice Walker that his grandfather secretly carried him away when he was five years old to have his faced ritually scarred. He said his face hurt and he cried and bled a lot, "but it was the surprise of it, the betrayal, that hurt most."[38] The deception and anger expressed here are also part of a Hopi Indian's description of his initiation:

> When the kachinas entered the kiva without masks, I had a great surprise. They were not spirits, but human beings. I recognized nearly every one of them and felt very unhappy, because I had been told all my life that the kachinas were gods. I was especially shocked and angry when I saw all my uncles, fathers, and clan brothers dancing as kachinas.[39]

Initiations—whether the ones described above or the Confirmations and Bar Mitzvahs with which the public is more familiar—typically require some unexpected physical, emotional, and/or mental ordeal that often results in a lasting bodily mark or memory. Instruction, too, as described by Bly, requires that one "get" what is being taught and "keep" it as a new part of his knowledge. An initiate must do, get, and keep something he was not expecting or aware of.[40]

He is typically surprised by and afraid of what he is told or has to do. He may have to memorize difficult, uninteresting material or perform unpleasant, embarrassing tasks. When not warned or prepared, he feels betrayed and, if not physically hurt, emotionally so; but to show such feelings is to fail the test. Even when one willingly participates in an initiation, one usually does so without complete knowledge of what will be expected. One obeys and surrenders to an authority to gain acceptance. To belong one gives up one's personal freedom. Having withstood the test of an initiation or instruction, one then expects others after him to endure the same as a condition for membership.[41]

In a comparative study of world religions, Ronald Green reports that "as elders impart the sacred knowledge needed to bring them to adulthood, initiands are often subjected to ritual afflictions and trials. Symbolic or real humiliations are thrust upon them. . . . Because of the shared hardships and common experience of intense comradeship and equality [in this phase of the initiation, it] remains a permanent feature in the lives of the ritual cohort."[42] But as Walker and the study by Kosmin and Lachman show, these bonds are not as permanent as commonly perceived. In another study of initiation rites, Tom Driver observes that "there is something terrifying, because motiveless, in ritual sacrifice." He finds that "most theories concerning ritual sacrifice serve to rationalize it by proposing that its roots lie in some socially useful activity, whether in the killing of wild prey, the slaughter of domesticated animals, the redirection of violence onto a substitute victim, the propitiation of a god, or what not." But all of these "motives have about them the aura of rationalizations, which is why none ever seems satisfactory, and the scholarly quest for the origins of sacrifice appears unending." Driver's own suggestion is that the motive has "nothing to do with any rational reason" for sacrifice, but "lies within performance itself," that is "with a desire to perform something absolute."[43]

When synonyms for "perform" (such as accomplish, achieve, exhibit, execute, perpetrate, produce, or settle) and for "absolute" (such as certain, decisive, definite, dominant, exclusive, independent, supreme, unchallengable, unquestioned, or final) are used to fatten Driver's last statement, we come to the thrust of the activities of the contemporary men's movement.[44] The movement does seem to be dominated by a desire to accomplish and settle via special rituals, gatherings, and marches a certain and exclusive definition of manhood rather than by a desire to engage in a process of questioning and examination that would open up and create a diverse definition or various definitions of manhood.[45]

ORGANIZING MEANINGFUL EXPERIENCE

Although I take issue with the current focus of the men's movement on initiation, myth, and pivotal gatherings, I also recognize and am grateful for some men's attention to examining, checking, and changing much of conventional male socialization. Robert Bly's emphasis on the following statement by Robert Moore underscores the seriousness with which they want to change father-son relationships: "If you're a young man and you're not being admired by an older man, you're being hurt."[46] But I want to take their call for older men to admire younger men a step further and say that such admiration requires fathers to be open to learning from and being changed by the young men whom they admire. Fathers need the mentoring *of* and initiating *by* their proto-gay sons.

My differences with Bly are illustrated by examples I take from two novels, E. M. Forster's *Maurice* and Hermann Hesse's *Siddhartha*. In Forster's novel, the proto-gay fatherless Maurice is taken aside by his well-intending male teacher for instruction about sex. The father-substitute ignores Maurice's confusion and inability to relate to his "scientific" explanation and persuades him to agree that sex and marriage with a woman is the "the crown of life." Because the explanation "bore no relation to his experiences," Maurice does not respond with "the kind of question" that boys had asked in the past. So the teacher quizzes him; and Maurice knows that he must demonstrate "a spurious intelligence, a surface flicker" of understanding. The teacher's relief and approval—"That's right. . . . You need never be puzzled or bothered now."—is, however, unsettled by Maurice's subsequent announcement, "I think I shall not marry." The teacher denies and ignores any truth to Maurice's claim and offers instead, "This day ten years hence—I invite you and your wife to dinner with my wife and me. Will you accept?" Flattered and pleased, Maurice accepts; but below the surface of their "bargain" Maurice despises the teacher and says to himself, "Liar, coward, he's told me nothing."[47]

Countering this monologic imposing of information is Siddhartha's encounter with Vasudeva, the ferryman, in Hesse's novel. The ferryman "rescues" or "saves" Siddhartha from despair and meaninglessness because he knew how to listen "with great attention":

> It was one of the ferryman's greatest virtues that, like few peo-ple, he knew how to listen. Without his saying a word, the speaker felt that Vasudeva took in every word, quietly, expec-tantly, that he missed nothing. He did not await anything with impatience and gave neither praise nor blame—he only listened. Siddhartha felt how wonderful it was to have such a listener who could be absorbed in another person's life, his strivings, his sor-rows.[48]

Unlike Maurice, who silently despises and condemns his teacher, Siddhartha thanks the ferryman "for listening so well. . . . I will also learn from you in this respect."[49] Knowing the difference between telling and listening—between telling a son what to be and listening to what he wants to be—is basic to understanding how to raise proto-gay kids.

DIALOGICAL GUIDANCE AND INITIATION

My concern about the flattening effect for proto-gay kids by a renewal of the initiating and mentoring role of fathers is based also on my own experience. My father was someone with whom I did spend long hours, and my father also took responsibility for instructing and initiating me. When I was twelve he told me about sex; and right before I turned fourteen he told me about masturbation. His candor, good intentions, and practice were indeed unusual compared to what my friends received from their fathers. I do not think there was any way for my father to know that by preparing and moving me into heterosexual adulthood he was scaring me into a prolonged and frightened silence. And this assumption of heterosexuality is the problem with initiations and rites of passage into manhood, because they are predicated on an understanding of manhood that does not allow for the shaping of manhood by the initiate or student. I worry that renewing the so-called traditional father role of initiator and mentor and the construction or renewal of rites of passage to manhood do not provide for ways to listen to and be informed by what Haraway refers to as the "halting voices" of proto-gay kids. The receiving and hearing of these voices are less likely to occur within a predetermined progression of rites of passage than within the familiarity of experience occasioned and structured by the interaction generated by everyday chores and errands done together.

Within such a continuum or process of time spent together—and much of it for me consisted of long boring hours as a go-fer for endless home repair and maintenance tasks—my father did sense and hear me out about what he could see concerned or troubled me. He did hear me out of my agonizing struggles with Little League baseball, out of his own enthusiasm for the sport, and into the discovery of my own preference for horseback riding lessons and his accompanying me to them. When watching football games he accurately read the shift in my attention from boredom to enthusiasm when the half-time baton twirlers came on. Together we bought a baton, and our backyard was as much a place for me to twirl it, as it was for my brother to organize the ever-present touch-football game.

By drawing attention to an ongoing process of simply being together, becoming increasingly familiar with each other, and sharing unplanned moments of salvation and by shying away from formal initiations into manhood, I do not wish to dismiss the need for guidance, initiation, and organization of meaningful father-son experience. I am proposing instead guidance and change as mutual and dialogical between father and son, not monological from father to son. I advocate refiguring the traditional father-son relationship so that rather than "prescribing" what a son should do, a father "researches"—goes out of his way to listen to—the needs and interests of his son and with him helps him meet his needs and solve his problems. When we take proto-gay kids seriously, we see that such guidance and initiation must be informed by what most fathers do not know from their own experience but can gain in a process in which they are receptive to their sons' input. My own optimism for such a process of familiarity comes from examples of my father's hearing, responding, and adjusting to me—of guiding me in response to what he was hearing from me.

An important event for my childhood—and one that I consider initiatory and guiding—was when our family went to a football game at the Yale Bowl, a special family outing. Known to my father, but not to me, was that when the half-time band came on the field, it would be lead by a male baton twirler. I learned later it was the reason for our going to this game at this time. He was providing me with a model that I needed but that he could not be and perhaps could not even understand.[50]

CARRYING, FERRYING,
SITTING, AND TALKING

The image and role of father that I shall propose and conclude with is that of the Ferryman from *Siddhartha*—the man in our life who by listening carries us along, carries us over. I shall take the term further into a wordplay (acknowledging that I am doing so in the translated English rather than the original German of the novel) and encourage fathers to be the Fairymen in their sons' lives—familiar, affectionate

men, who do not impress and change us with their great size or great
deeds, but by their listening, by the ease and lightness of their movement into our lives, and whose magic is in their readiness to change
themselves, to be changed by us, for the sake of our becoming.

My father died when I was fifteen years old. I regret that we could
not be together as I grew into adulthood and he into old age. I still
miss him and actually find myself thinking about him and missing
him more as I grow older. The way he related to me—his patience, his
close listening to me, his interest in whatever mattered to me, his response to and involvement in whatever activity preoccupied me at the
time—remains for me the standard by which I try to relate to my students as a professor and chaplain. I remember especially that he not
only cared for me and made me happy, but that being involved in my
life made him happy.

One small event in particular stays with me: My father and I had
been working on making shelves for my expanding collection of
horse statuettes, but our work was interrupted by the Christmas holidays. On Christmas Day, we went to my aunt's for the traditional dinner and get-together of our extended family, but right after the meal
instead of hanging around as usual, my father said that he and I were
going home to finish the shelves we had been working on. I chuckle
now when I think that perhaps my father may have simply wanted an
excuse to get away from the madhouse of cleaning up, kids running
around, noise, and family gossip. But what I remember most clearly
is the soaring fullness of pride and specialness that I felt as my father
and I left everyone else behind and walked home together to work on
our project. That such a simple act of attention has the power to make
an important difference in a person's life is what I try to remember as
I go about my work of relating to students. To offer dramatic, groundbreaking, programmatic advice and direction is much less important
than simply listening closely to everyday needs and responding with
practical, caring acts.

My father was not an educated man. He was a tool-and-die maker
by trade and worked in the factory in our town. My parents told my
brother and me many times that they had been accepted by colleges
after high school but could not afford to attend—their way of letting
us know that the same would not happen to us, especially if we
worked hard in school and saved our earnings from summer and

weekend jobs. My father was taking night courses in the hopes of getting a college degree when he was diagnosed with heart disease.

After he was diagnosed and told how long he could expect to live, he talked with me about death. He told me that the best way to honor and love him after he died would to be to get on with life and to do well in school. He also said that right after he died I should not worry about doing what people expected me to do, in other words that I did not have to observe the conventions of mourning if I did not want to. This advice was important because before and after the funeral I was uncomfortable at home with all the comings and goings of people and I wanted to be in school instead. Although some friends and teachers thought I should not be back at school so soon, I did not care what they thought. Many times since then I have marveled at how skillfully he anticipated the difficulties I would encounter and guided me through them. Such anticipation was based on how well he had gotten to know and respond to me during all the ordinary time we had spent together.

Of course, I have also wondered how we might have gotten along later in life and how he might have responded to my coming out as a gay man. I imagine that he would have gotten through his own biases, recognized my need to be open, and helped me in the process of coming to terms with defying convention. My mother and her second husband did respond in that manner, so I do not think I am idealizing what my father's response might have been. I also sometimes wonder if I romanticize my father and the way he raised me, but my search for unpleasant, negative, or harmful words and deeds on his part produces nothing. My parents were able to be both strict and permissive without depriving or spoiling us. They were fair and clear about their expectations. They explained, talked, and listened. Although my friends were often spanked, grounded, or denied their allowances for misbehaving, I cannot remember my parents threatening us or using such punishment. The enduring lesson that I learned from them was to treat people the way I wanted them to treat me. Even if others did not reciprocate, I was taught that I should be the one to hold to and live by the standard and that doing so would give me the certainty to navigate through conflicts, disagreement, and disapproval.

I know that a lot of gay people have not had the advantage of having parents who understand and support them. Many had loving parents when they were children but have lost that love after coming out. As we listen to and "activate" the previously "limited voices" of proto-gay kids we hear and find answers to more than their own specific problems and injuries. Their need for the company of their fathers—for their "love, acceptance, and support"—expresses as well the needs of other kids. By listening to proto-gay kids we hear the words that rescue other kids, that provide answers to what they need and want, that inform and change how we relate to kids in general. By listening to them we find connections to other kids. Their words open us up and spark us to question our preconceived and unexamined ways of relating to children. Perhaps proto-gay kids have traditionally been so overlooked because their needs brings us face to face with the needs of all kids. By ignoring their knowledge of how we should relate to them, we overlook an important resource for knowing how to relate to all our children.

Chapter 2

Learning from and with Children

UNDERLYING RELIGIOUS PRINCIPLE

When I began my doctoral studies in social ethics at Union Seminary in New York City, I needed a part-time job. I wanted my job to have some relevance and application to my studies, so I looked at various positions offered through the field education office at the Seminary. The one that I applied for was at the Seminary's own day care center. Previously I had taught elementary and high school, but I had not worked with preschool children. During my residency in the doctoral program, I was employed as an assistant teacher in the infant-toddler room of the day care center. For a few hours each day I would leave classes, assignments, and research behind and become involved in the various tasks of caring for young children. I also began to integrate my job into my studies by taking courses in early childhood education at Columbia University's Teachers College, which is across the street from Union.

When a full-time position of head teacher in the nursery room opened, I applied and was hired. The search committee of parents was so impressed by my previous work in the infant-toddler room and by my willingness to take courses in early childhood education that they decided to give me primary responsibility for caring for their three-to-four-year-olds. During the next year, I was engaged in early childhood education as both a teacher and a scholar. My academic study of the educational needs of young children and my job as a teacher in the day care center to meet those needs reinforced, affected, and shaped each other. What I learned then and there has affected my work as a college chaplain and professor more than any other academic or professional experience. The way I learned to approach young children, what I could and should expect to give to and receive from them, and what my role should be in their learning experiences directly affect the way I approach, relate to, and interact with college students.

Underlying what I learned is a principle found in much religious thinking. In Taoism, for example, the Chinese term for "nonaction," *wu wei,* means allowing everything to do what it naturally does so that its nature will be satisfied. It does not mean doing nothing or keeping silent, but finding a way to let others do what they can do best.[1] The Christian educator John Westerhoff also warns against "the tendency to inflict on children adult ways of being in the world"; simply being with children in their work and play is difficult because "we always seem to want to do something to or for them so they will be like us or like what we would like to be." Westerhoff says that even though "it is easier to impose than reflect, easier to instruct than to share, easier to act than to interact, . . . to be with a child . . . means self-control more than child-control." From a Christian perspective, education "cannot be a vehicle for control; it must encourage an equal sharing of life in community."[2] So, too, does the Jewish theologian Marc Ellis recognize what he calls the ongoing "tension between empire and community." "Empire" represents our "attempt to dominate, control, or manipulate others" and our "creation of structures that ensure a pattern of dominance and control." "Community," on the other hand, represents "equality, cooperation, and mutuality in decision making" and "the goals, and structures . . . that foster creativity rather than domination."[3] When speaking of how to create and build such community, the Vietnamese Buddhist monk Thich Nhat Hanh says, "if we want to live in peace and happiness with a person, we have to see the suchness of that person," and he uses the word "suchness" to mean "the essence," "particular characteristics," or "true nature" of a person.[4] Working with young children should be about helping them to develop and follow through with their own interests, needs, and feelings. Instead of trying to put something of ourselves into children, we should be drawing them out of themselves.

Contemporary early childhood education in the West is itself rooted in an emphasis on "the inherent goodness of children, the spontaneous nature of development, and the importance of deriving educational practices from children's natural interests," as reflected in the ideas of such early educational reformers as John Amos Comenius (1592-1670), Jean-Jacques Rousseau (1712-1778), and Johann Heinrich Pestalozzi (1746-1827).[5] But good ideas do not necessarily reflect and ensure good practice. Just as Westerhoff acknowledges the difficulty of simply being with children and Ellis recognizes the tension between our wanting to control and cooperate with others, so does Thich Nhat Hanh realize that living in peace and happiness is not easy, because we cannot "expect a person always to be a flower," and "we have to understand his or her garbage as well."[6] From the earliest efforts to formalize early childhood education in the nineteenth century, ideas about the inherent goodness, spontaneous nature, and natural interests of children have often been generated by what adults want and expect children to do and be rather than by what children are interested in—especially when their interests upset or displease us.

As I studied the work of those who founded major movements and approaches in early childhood education, I learned as much from their mistakes as I did from their progressive ideas and practices. From their mistakes I formed a cautionary ethic of how not to interact with students and of what to look out for and guard against. I shall begin with the pioneers of early childhood education: Frederick Froebel in Germany, Maria Montessori in Italy, and John Dewey, G. Stanley Hall, Edward Thorndike, and Patty Smith Hill in the United States; then I shall shift to the second wave of theorists: Jean Piaget in Switzerland, Jerome Bruner in the United States, and Susan Isaacs in Great Britain. Finally, I shall discuss my response to and application of their theories in my work at Union Seminary's Day Care Center.

THE PIONEERS: NINETEENTH
AND EARLY TWENTIETH CENTURIES

Frederick Froebel's view of children as innately good and born with all that is necessary to understand the universe was linked to his belief in cosmic truths and spiritual unity. He designed a sequence of exercises for children that were intended to symbolize the innerconnectedness of all life and to release and unfold a child's inner powers and ability to understand. Precisely formulated, ordered, and accompanied by prescribed, ready-made materials, the exercises were to be demonstrated by a teacher and imitated by the children. A child was to grow or unfold by completing the set of exercises, each of which required a series of manipulations that foreshadowed the next exercise and summarized the previous ones.

Whereas Froebel's approach mirrored his belief in fixed truths and universal laws, newer movements turned to direct observation of children for their insights. G. Stanley Hall's Child Study Movement, for example, by paying greater attention to children's bodies, observed that large muscles develop before small muscles and accordingly emphasized free play over Froebel's small hand-manipulating exercises. John Dewey and the American Progressive Movement developed a curriculum in response to children's needs as discerned through direction interaction with and observation of children's daily experiences.

Dewey moved away from Froebel's ready-made, hand-manipulative materials to an ongoing restructuring of the whole learning environment. Dewey's classroom could be rearranged so that it could become, for example, either a make-believe fire station or grocery store, while Froebel's classroom needed tables and chairs fixed in place. Dewey's children learned through participation and discovery, not through imitation. Everyday problems were brought forth and solved by the children. Careful planning was necessary but left room for the unexpected. Froebel's sequence of activities, on the other hand, did not allow for variation. His teacher was the unquestioned director. Dewey's teacher was more of a guide and facilitator who observed, identified, and planned around the children's inquiries and concerns.

In Italy, Maria Montessori's design for a spontaneous, natural process of education drew on scientific techniques and theories of behavior from developmental psychology.[7] Like Froebel, she was concerned with how a child develops the powers with which he or she is endowed by nature, but her emphasis was cognitive, not spiritual. She saw early childhood learning not as a spiritual unfolding but as preacademic preparation for reading, writing, and arithmetic. "Motor" exercises, which children perform "naturally," such as walking, sitting, carrying objects, and water play, were important for developing work habits and responsibility, such as watering plants and understanding that this activity ensures their survival and growth. "Sensory" exercises, on the other hand, involved elaborate ready-made instructional materials of varying forms, sizes, colors, weights, temperatures, sounds, and textures that developed techniques of observation, discrimination, and decision making. She observed that the critical development of sensory-motor coordinations occurred from three to six years of age and were preparatory for and prototypic of the kind of matching, recognition, and identification basic to all academic learning.

Unlike Dewey's environment, which was restructured in an ongoing interaction among children around their interests, Montessori's was designed and prepared once and for all as the best of all possible educational environments for what children could learn and accomplish at a particular age. The prepared environment was an organized and coordinated set of materials and equipment from which a child could select what suited him or her at any time and proceed with it at his or her self-imposed rate. But eventually all children were directed and required to use the same materials in proper sequence, and there was one right way to use the materials in the prepared environment. The sequence of activities was derived from "developmental" psychology (i.e., in accordance with that which a child could by nature and age accomplish and in which he or she could take pleasure). By 1915, in the United States, however, a new thrust in early childhood education came from "behavioral" psychology, especially from the work of Edward Thorndike.[8]

Thorndike's "laws of learning" set the task of the educator as making changes in the human being via habit formation. The teacher provided an appropriate stimulus to build desired responses. Learning was a process by which responses became more efficient and economical. Stimulus-response psychology emphasized the plasticity of the child. By advising teachers to "put together what you wish to put together," to "reward good impulses," and conversely to "keep apart what you wish to have separate" and "let undesireable impulses bring discomfort,"[9] Thorndike gave teachers the role of master designers responsible for modifying children's behavior. He emphasized the need for teachers to pay attention to a child's readiness, enthusiasm, and motivation as a prerequisite for learning. At Teachers College in New York City, Patty Smith Hill used an eclectic approach to foster moral training through social interaction. Like Dewey, she used the experiences and interests of the children to initiate classroom activities; however, Dewey's cooperation and sharing, with the help of Thorndike's development of habit formation, became a goal, a preferred manner of behaving, a good habit, rather than a process for problem solving.[10]

The theories and approaches of these pioneers of early childhood education represented and drew their credibility and support from the intellectual and cultural movements of their day. In the time of each, progressive thinking and its emerging set of principles came to occupy a dominant position of belief through its application to various realms of human activity. Society was changed or affected by each movement and subsequently approved, integrated, and protected it. Romanticism, Democratic Idealism, and Scientific Empiricism were such movements, and early childhood education was one of the realms of human activity to which they were applied.

Froebel embraced early nineteenth-century romanticism, Dewey embraced late nineteenth-century and early twentieth-century democracy, and Montessori, Hall, and Thorndike embraced empirically based science. Each of the theorists approached early childhood education with a belief in, support of, and adherence to the principles and values of a movement or school of thought. Froebel's perception of children as having hidden powers that should be unfolded was consonant with nineteenth-century romantic thought; Dewey's perception of children as individual members of a group or minisociety based on sharing and cooperation was the view of a turn-of-the-century democrat; and Montessori's perception that through careful observation one could know and educate children was typical of the empirical scientist of the early twentieth century. Their theories did not begin with nor emerge from the experiences of children but were applied to them. The theories tended more to shape than to be shaped by children's experiences.

For today's work of developing child-initiated learning, however, key contributions from each of the pioneering theorists can be identified and used. Froebel's insight that children like to play and manipulate objects within their environments remains central for respecting and working with children's preferences. Empirical observation, especially when frequent and periodic, is critical for gaining information about children and for updating and checking adults' perceptions of children. Dewey's emphasis on the ongoing restructuring of the environment is necessary for children to participate in and to determine their activities and growth. Behaviorism, in providing the insight that children can readily change, brings us face-to-face with our power and responsibility as adults to influence and shape children. We are reminded that whatever we do, even if it be indifference or avoidance, will have some effect.

Another reason for appraising the work of these pioneers is that Dewey, Montessori, and Thorndike foreshadowed subsequent approaches in early childhood education that remain dominant today. Montessori's work set in motion an educational focus on developmental psychology that was expanded and changed through Jean Piaget's work in Switzerland. Behaviorism would find a modern-day theorist in Jerome Bruner in the United States. Dewey's attention to children's needs and interests would be extended in Great Britain by Susan Isaacs.

THE SECOND WAVE:
MID-TWENTIETH CENTURY

Jean Piaget observed that children interact with the external environment through "adaptation," which he saw as the essential intellectual function. From birth a child tries to achieve a state of equilibrium by balancing what is new with what is already known. Through observing, questioning, and probing, a teacher could create a situation of disequilibrium for a child that would yield new understanding. Piaget claimed that children moved through stages that mark significant logical progressive changes in how they achieve equilibrium. The theoretical framework within which Piaget made his empirical observations was biological determinism.

Underlying his approach was the assumption that mental growth was similar to the linearity and predictability of biological growth, and that it could, therefore, be anticipated and charted. Piaget regarded children's intellectual development much as a biologist would regard a plant's growth. One could study many plants of a particular species, generalize from the findings to the species as a whole, and then know what to expect from other plants of this kind. If expectations were not met, one could conclude that something was lacking, such as adequate water, sunlight, or fertile soil. Children who did not progress to appropriate developmental stages were seen as requiring a situation of disequilibrium to which they would adapt intellectually. A teacher, therefore, set goals for the children determined by the teacher's observation of what the child needed to make the next intellectual transition.[11]

Piaget's contribution to developing a child-centered and child-initiated curriculum is the primacy he assigned to observing children. By studying the child, stage-relevant activities were designed and planned for him or her. The effect of child observation was enhanced because teachers worked in small groups and paid attention to individuals and how each child was working. Piaget rejected predetermined and "closed teaching" materials, which he considered the great weakness of Montessori's approach: "Take, for example, lining things up in order of length. She started with a fine idea, but she ended up with form boards! Each piece fits in its place, and that's as far as you can go. Whereas, in fact, you can order all sorts of different things."[12]

Piaget was primarily concerned with how children think, while Jerome Bruner was concerned with how children learn. Bruner saw learning as connecting the external with the internal or bringing an outside body of knowledge inside the self and understanding it. He said that any body of knowledge, whether it be zoology, the history of transportation, cooking, or mathematics, had a basic structure or logic that could be appropriately presented to any age group through one or all of three modes—enactic, iconic, and symbolic—of representing that body of knowledge. The basic structure of cooking, for example, might be grasped by a young child through the enactic mode of "body-action learning," such as stirring, mixing, and pouring, that subsequently could be extended by the more complicated iconic mode of "learning through images," such as with pictures and pictorial recipes that would show and tell a child how to cook. Next, the symbolic mode of "learning through language" would explain and discuss cooking in terms of its laws, propositions, and principles, such as boiling, evaporation, and various other ways of transforming food substances. Being able to comprehend a body of knowledge by listening to a teacher talk about it indicated more advanced learning than being able only to participate physically in it.

For Bruner, the structure for learning anything lay in the body of knowledge itself and educators had to know what the structure was and create an appropriate inner structure in children to match it. Intellectual growth depended on internalizing events into a "storage system" that corresponded to the environment. Teachers paid attention to motivation and readiness and consciously used rewards and punishments as they guided children with a prescribed discovery method through a particular body of knowledge. The sequence of instruction was teacher-directed and the body of knowledge was teacher-chosen.

Bruner's work would not seem to be a helpful resource for minimizing adult imposition and maximizing children's initiation, participation, and autonomy. However, he did provide some insights into what the other seemingly more helpful approaches neglected. Commenting on the American Progressive Movement founded by Dewey, Bruner offered an apt criticism:

> A generation ago, the progressive movement urged that knowledge be related to the child's own experience and brought out of the realm of empty abstractions. A good idea was translated into banalities about the home, then the friendly postman and trashman, then the community and so on. It is a poor way to compete with the child's own dramas and mysteries.[13]

Bruner thought that children should be introduced to the unusual through visual material, discussion, and activities related to people and cultures outside of what children encountered every day.

He noticed from his interviews with children that they discovered "kinship and likeness in what at first seemed bizarre, exotic, and even a little repellent."[14] In other words, he found "that to personalize knowledge one does not simply link it to the familiar."[15] For example, Bruner described an incident when children were viewing a film of an Eskimo family in which a young boy stones a gull to death:

> Our children watched, horror-struck. One girl, Kathy, blurted out, "He's not even human, doing that to the seagull." The class was silent. Then another girl, Jennine, said quietly: "He's got to grow up to be a hunter. His mother was smiling when he was doing that." And then an extended discussion about how people have to do things to learn how to feel appropriately. "What would you do if you had to live there? Would you be as smart

about getting along as they are with what they've got?" said one boy going back to the accusation that Alexei was inhuman to stone the bird.[16]

Bruner then went on to say that the children were not learning about seagulls and Eskimos as much as they were about their own feelings and preconceptions that, until then, were too implicit to be self-recognized.

While Bruner offered a valid critique of the American Progressive Movement, he also missed providing an adequate solution. Whereas the Progressive Movement imposed an adult view of the familiar upon children, Bruner imposed an adult view of the unfamiliar. In both cases, the children did what was expected of them. They could pretend to be letter carriers as well as they could empathize with children in strange and faraway situations. Children have adapted to the various educational approaches that adults have designed throughout the history of early childhood education. Children completed the complicated exercises designed by Froebel, conformed to the environment designed by Montessori, and provided the response desired by adherents to behavioral theory. Bruner's claim that children got beyond their initial disgust after discussing and becoming familiar with the bizarre subject matter in the film says little more than that children also learn to play doctor in a Deweyan classroom that has been equipped with props from the medical professions.

The key to understanding why both Bruner's and Dewey's approaches manipulated children and imposed learning rather than encouraged children and facilitated learning can be found in Bruner's comment about the shortcoming of the Progressive Movement: "It is a poor way to compete with the child's own dramas and mysteries." Neither the Progressive Movement nor Bruner began with those dramas and mysteries. The Progressive Movement sought to tame them, to cast them in the culturally specific trappings of the democratic neighborhood. Bruner sought to upstage them, "to compete" with them by fashioning presentations that would shock and confront. Bruner's approach tried to provide a stimulus that would elicit a particular response. He sought to bring forth certain feelings, but he did not begin with those feelings. He did not attempt to find out what children felt and how they might want to function in a number of self-selected contexts, but only as they responded to the particular subject matter that the teacher chose to present to them. Bruner controlled children's feelings by his choice of material and how it was presented to the children. He reduced and controlled the range of experiences and emotions that could be expressed in the classroom. In both Bruner's and Dewey's approaches adults wanted children to respond and perform in a prescribed manner (i.e., to empathize with an unfamiliar situation or to function democratically within a small group.) Both approaches began with trying to make children be or do something. Neither began with how children feel, what they want and need, and in what they are interested.

Susan Isaacs, however, not only focused on children's feelings and encouraged their expression, she found that "affect is the bedrock of cognition." Isaacs had two broad educational aims. The first was "to stimulate the active inquiry of children themselves rather than to 'teach' them." Unlike Bruner, whose teacher was to organize a body of knowledge for the children, Isaacs sought to assist children to organize their own bodies of knowledge. Her second aim was "to bring within children's immediate experience every range of fact to which their interests reached out." Unlike Bruner, she did not select a body of knowledge, bring it to children, and then match them to it. Instead, she sought to find out what children wanted to learn, to help them to do it, and to push beyond what they already knew.[17]

She provides the following example from her Maltinghouse School:

> The children had taken to modelling in plasticine whole scenes of places they had been to, such as the bathing-pool on the river, with the people in it. One day whilst they were modeling some such subject, an aeroplane passed over the garden, as often happened. The children all watched it, and shouted to it as they usually did, "Come down, come down!" But one of them remarked that the man in the plane "can't hear us because of the noise the engine is making." Another said, "Perhaps he can see us?" And another, "I wonder what he sees, what we look like." I then suggested, "Perhaps we could make a model of the garden as it looks to the man in the plane?" This suggestion delighted them. We began on it at once, and put several days' work into it. Some of the children climbed "as high up on the ladder as we

can get, to see how it looks from the plane." One boy of four-and-a-half realized spontaneously that from the plane only the tops of their own heads would be seen, and he dotted a number of small flat ovals over the paths of the model, "That's the children running about." The children talked of the relative sizes of the different garden plots, the trees and lawns and buildings, and ran out to compare them several times. Presently I showed them an aerial photograph of a countryside with trees and houses and roads. They discussed this eagerly, and suggested modelling [their own area and town] "as the man in the plane sees it." I gave them a simplified map of [the town], and after long discussion of this, and tracing of the river and the streets and roads which they knew, we drew one of our own together.

And when, presently, I told the children that I was going to cycle to a place I had not been to before, and one of them said, "Then how will you know the way?" another answered, "She'll look at the map." And another said, "Yes, it's when you come to the cross-roads that you'll have to look at the map—it'll be all right when you're going along a straight road, but when you come to where the roads divide, you'll have to get out your map and look.[18]

Because the children were fascinated by what was happening around them, she appropriated the familiar as a means to the unfamiliar and the unknown. For Isaacs the origin of learning lay in children's interests and proceeded by means of their interactions with one another, with teachers (more than one), with other school personnel, and with various outside community members as required by children's self-initiated projects—"A question from one child as to what 'wood is made of' led to a visit to a small mill to see the tree trunks sawed into planks."

Teachers became part of projects by contributing information and helping children to think through problems, but as a resource, participant, and equal more than as an authority. She warned, however, that the behavior of children will always have some reference to what adults expect—"An adult who is there with children cannot . . . create conditions so 'free' that they rule out his prestige as an adult."[19] Even a teacher who aims to be passive gives messages of either silent endorsement or noninterest. "The use of the children's identification with grown-ups and their readiness to feel that what we do is a desireable thing to do, was one of the regular ways of introducing them to new interests, or of influencing them towards sustained effort in any direction." Teachers who do not want to influence children in an authoritarian manner will use their "prestige" as adults to stimulate the active inquiry of the children themselves. The impulse of a teacher will be both to teach and learn from the child, to be a guide as well as a fellow worker and playmate.[20]

Isaacs sought to discover a child's interests and experiences, rather than to ascertain his or her intellectual readiness. She criticized Piaget's theory of intellectual maturation because it put forth a "pseudo-biological sequence" with "the rigid formality of a logical system" that did not allow "that different levels of functioning occur alongside each other." While she agreed that development showed a coherence of growth, she maintained that it was a psychological coherence having "the elasticity and vital movement of a living process . . . into which experience is taken up more and more." One stage does not give way to another as much as "there is a progressive penetration of feeling and phantasy by experience, a progressive ordering by relational thought of the child's responses to the world." She said that by stressing the mental maturation of children as a "a literal organic fact (of the same order of the facts of embryology)," we both "under-estimate the part played by experience in their development" and "over-emphasize the difference between children and ourselves," because we see them only as not as developed as ourselves.[21]

Isaacs advocated that adults share experiences with children because her own research and her study of psychoanalysis showed that the general modes of thought of little children are not fundamentally different from those of adults. The "essential action of cognition" for a child and an adult lies in educing, bringing out, and drawing forth understanding, reasoning, and practical organization from relations that are directly apprehended and experienced. Adults are not superior intellectually to children, only more or differently experienced. What limits a child is not an inability to apprehend the relationship between things and/or people, but an inability to deal with complex ideas. Adults know about and can introduce children to new experiences. But children also have experiences that adults do not have, did not have, or cannot remember without sharing those experiences with children. Isaacs reminded teachers that working with children did not mean prescribing experiences for them, but listening to their interests and suggesting new experiences to help them develop their interests.[22]

RESPONSE AND APPLICATION

The staff at my day care center found Isaacs' approach attractive and useful; however, we applied some caution in our application of it. We realized that when adults listen to or observe children, they may not be ready to accept what they do not like or what goes against their preferred approach to and understanding of children. Rather than working with and from the child's interests or needs, they may dismiss or divert them and rationalize what they do not like as inappropriate for learning. Some of Isaacs' observations reveal her own personal bias and her unexamined acceptance and application of Sigmund Freud's theories. For example, she reports that one five-year-old boy "is always very fond of bead necklaces, ear-rings and bracelets, which he makes for himself, of fastening coloured ribbons of a hair slide on his hair, and in general, behaving rather more like a girl than a boy." Even though Isaacs claims that her study is for "the scientific public" and that her observations are "systematic" rather than "incidental," her use of inflated modifiers ("always very"), evaluative rather than descriptive terms ("fond of" rather than "plays with"), and stereotypical judgment ("more like a girl than a boy") do not conform to scientific standards. Freud's notions of the Oedipal conflict and of masculinity and femininity influence her observations of the boy and the conclusion she draws from them: "it seems likely" that such an "exaggerated and consistent feminine attitude, at this age" is "by no means always apparent in ordinary life" and represents a "regression" to an earlier "normal phase of feminine identification" that has been "re-awakened . . . when genital rivalry with the father for the love of the mother has been over-strongly stimulated by one situation or another." Even if such a rivalry does exist, her view and characterization of it is not consistent. At one time, she interprets the boy's "hostile expressions" during play with other children as representing a rivalry "with his mother in relation to the father" and, at another time, as "rivalry with the father for the mother." She tends, too, to single out and accent this boy's behavior. A review of her reported data shows that all of the children frequently express hostility to the teachers, but she emphasizes his as "strong open hostility" and links it to an aversion to women, even though the latter is sustained only by the fact that all of the teachers happen to be women. Although the appeal of Isaacs's approach to early childhood education lies in her usual avoidance of predetermined and generalized categories to measure and evaluate children's behavior, she apparently succumbed and resorted to such categories when faced with what she did not understand, approve of, or regard as positive or normal. Her professed openness "to meet the spontaneous inquiries of the children . . . and give them means of following these inquiries out" diminished in the face of what was either unacceptable to her or constrained by Freudian theory. Not unlike the other educators discussed earlier, Isaacs sometimes succumbed to interpreting children's experiences through the filter of her preferred school of thought rather than always beginning with those experiences and letting them shape her theory.[23]

Our staff found that what was missing from Isaacs' theory was a provision for ongoing critical evaluation of the teachers' personally felt and culturally imposed biases, values, and norms. To maintain an ongoing evaluation of our responses to the children we developed an interactive team approach. We thought that a staff of teachers reflecting variety in race, gender, sexual orientation, age, and ethnicity was necessary to identify, discuss, and challenge teachers' biases. For the twenty-two children there were four teachers present in the classroom at all times. The full-time teaching staff, consisting of one thirty-five-year-old black woman, one thirty-two-year-old white woman, and one forty-year-old white gay man, was given greater variety by the employment of four work-study students from the seminary—all in their twenties—one black man, two black women, and one white lesbian—to fill the fourth teacher's position on a rotating basis. In hiring substitute teachers we recruited people who were older and represented the racial and ethnic populations of the immediate neighborhood.

The benefits of the staff's diversity were revealed in several ways: The younger work-study teachers were more open to extending popular television shows into creative inquiry, whereas older teachers tended to reject the shows and their possibility for building on and from the familiar. Lesbian and gay teachers showed others that by viewing children's relationships through heterosexual filters, the staff imposed patterns and models of relationships on the children. They pointed out that with subtle cues adults reinforce what is familiar and taken for granted by them. For example, some teachers would view an affectionate relationship between a boy and girl as romantic or loving, while that between boys or between girls was seen as friendly. They might playfully tease a boy by asking, "Who's your new girl-friend?" but would never think to ask, "Who's your new boyfriend?" When the gay male teacher pointed out that two boys in the classroom were developing a close, nurturing relationship that seemed more romantic than friendly, other teachers were a bit shocked and put off. Only after he challenged the staff and discussed this issue with them did the classroom become a environment in which these two boys could have the time, occasions, and recognition they needed to devote to each other.

As if verifying Isaacs' view of "affect as the bedrock of cognition," these two boys launched into a period of creative inquiry, building projects, and cooperative problem-solving that had not happened until the staff acknowledged to themselves the commitment of these two boys to each other, the value of their relationship, and the time they should have together to nurture and develop their relationship. Most important, however, the staff realized from this discussion and experience that adults should not attribute adultlike relationships to children. We should not simply enlarge our understanding of children's relationships to embrace both heterosexual and gay/lesbian possibilities. What we need, instead, is to be ready to accept and value expressions of affection and interest not identical to our own. By openly sharing their own experiences with one another, as the gay male teacher had done, staff members were better able to understand the need for variety and inclusivity, but they also realized that they had to see beyond those experiences. They had to challenge one another to see beyond what was familiar to them and to help children develop relationships according to their own needs and interests. While the gay teacher's observation was the occasion to recognize and facilitate the relationship between the two boys in a way that was in the boys' interest, the staff came to understand also that they should not simply limit the boys' relationship to predetermined adult categories—"heterosexual" and "gay/lesbian." The point was not to understand the boys' relationship as romantic or friendly, gay or straight, but to see it for what it was from the point of view of the boys' needs, interests, and preferences. One's own experience should not be imposed on another person's experience, but rather should be a guide or filter through which one can see, recognize, compare, and respect different experiences. To consider one's experience in the context of others' experience should let us recognize and validate their experiences and not set our own above and apart from them. In this case, the gay teacher did not use his experience to label and understand the relationship as gay or similar to his own gay relationships, but he was able to recognize that an "unusual" or "special" relationship was not being given the seriousness and attention by the staff that it needed to develop on its own terms.

We were helped in realizing that the signals we gave to children were subtle and yet powerful when Beginning Equal,[24] a New-York-City-based training project working on issues of sexism and racism in early childhood education, offered to observe and monitor our interactions with the children. Observers were able to point out to us ways in which we responded differently to boys and girls without being aware of doing so. We spent more time with boys, we tended to help them settle their conflicts and to let the girls settle theirs by themselves, and we engaged boys in play that was more physically demanding. This tool for self-evaluation let us see the ways in which we might be encouraging and reinforcing social roles and behaviors at the expense of a child's own interests and needs. We tried to differentiate between those interests that a child acquired through social and cultural influences and those that were particular to her or him.

We attempted to create a culturally nonspecific, transformable, child-initiated environment in our traditional nursery school-type housekeeping area. The staff had been observing for a while that the quality of the dramatic play in this area imitated popular television shows. To provide an environment that would encourage dramatic play that was less culturally specific and copied, the staff changed the housekeeping area. Hand-me-down clothes were replaced with varying sizes, colors, prints, and weaves of fabric. The scaled-down, child-size simulated furniture—dining room table, stove, sink, refrigerator—was replaced with wooden boxes, boards, and crates that could be arranged to serve many "pretend" purposes. A climbing apparatus—four feet by four feet by four feet—was placed in the center with draping material in the form of four large sheets—six feet by four feet and made of purple, green, yellow, and red parachute cloth. The apparatus had two inner levels that could be moved up and down. Compared with the previous setup, more children now used the area with greater occupancy at one time, they resolved conflict and competition for materials among themselves, and adult supervision was not required as much. The children created their own quiet time and secret places that were respected by others. The child-determined ethic that emerged in this area seemed to be one of communal privacy and relaxation—a place to be oneself in the company of others. Clothes were designed by draping and tying the various fabrics, and teachers were often asked for or offered to help. Activities were more child-created than copied from television shows. The staff had to remind themselves, however, that perhaps the children were simply meeting staff's expectations that were subtly, but nonetheless strongly communicated. Through subsequent participation, observation, and evaluation, we realized that we should also recognize the possibilities for extending and working from popular television shows rather than ignoring and replacing them.

We noticed that one boy had shifted from disinterest in a popular muscle-hero cartoon series to enthusiastic imitation of the featured character. Because many of the other boys engaged each other in excited conversations about the previous night's episode, we thought that this boy might be trying to belong and to satisfy peer expectations. We learned from his mother that he could not sit through an episode of the show without getting up and pursuing other activities, such as listening to music, dancing, or reading, but each day at school he announced his arrival by bounding into the classroom with a robust leap like that of the show's superhero. Although the staff initially saw his behavior as the result of having made a choice against his own real interests and modes of expression, we also needed to understand his interest in group approval and acceptance. We turned our attention, therefore, not to steering him away from modeling his behavior after the show, but to exploring other ways that children could announce themselves if they chose as they entered the classroom each day. By focusing on the need to be noticed, we were able to plan frequent opening group-time exercises during which children could introduce themselves by demonstrating or talking about something occurring in their lives outside of school. Because teachers knew about their outside lives through ongoing conversations with their parents, they could suggest various new ways to introduce themselves, such as with props, drawings, photos, stories, and songs from home. Imitations of superheroes took their place alongside of other introductions as children felt encouraged to share their experiences with others.

The staff members also found it necessary to discuss and weigh their enthusiasm in indiscriminately using nonsexist and nonracist materials that were becoming popular as early childhood education professionals examined the impact of racial, cultural, and gender-role stereotyping on children's development. For example, the staff initially welcomed the book *William's Doll* by Charlotte Zolotow[25] as an effective resource for helping children to question "boy" and "girl" activities and to express feelings that were constrained by sex-role socialization. The story is about a boy who wants a doll to love and care for and who maintains his interest and desire through his brother's teasing and his father's disapproval. William's grandmother eventually arrives to help him purchase the doll and to reason with the father.

The staff found that reading the book to the children was powerful. The following day usually saw a large increase in doll-playing by the boys—an increase that subsided by the next day. The staff evaluated this abrupt start and finish of activity by examining the book more closely. We noticed that it contains two major provisions for William to qualify as an appropriate carer of dolls. The first is that he is very good at basketball and very clever in setting up his electric train set. The second is the grandmother's explanation that William needed a doll with which to practice parenting, because someday he would be a father. The staff realized that the book is more of an apology for than encouragement of children's feelings. It caught the attention of the boys because it addresses a sensitive, neglected, and pressing concern for many of them—the need to express nurturing feelings—but it compromised those feelings. The book does not simply describe and celebrate those feelings. It makes a deal with boys in terms of a trade-off to satisfy certain cultural values and expectations.

We felt that the reasons boys want to play with dolls may have little to do with wanting to be fathers. William himself never says he wants to be one. Nor should boys feel less deserving of doll-play if they are not athletically or mechanically proficient, as the book depicts William. The book offers conditions under which feelings that are socially perceived as "odd" may be expressed, and the conditions are that a boy who plays with dolls not be a sissy, not grow up to be a nonparent or gay, and not be abnormal in other behaviors and feelings.

The staff found that the book pretended to change certain stereotypes and values, but ended up affirming them. And the boys in our classroom, as the staff observed, took relief at first hearing the message, but could not follow through for long because controls were imposed on their feelings that were little different from the controls that they had previously felt. The book seems to maintain an abiding fear that boys may veer too much from what is expected of them. For the staff, *William's Doll* was an opportunity to critique our own best intentions to provide and impose nonsexist child care standards.

We continued to examine and evaluate our tendency to impose sex-role socialization on children rather than to free them from it. For example, group music time was an opportunity to make traditional and familiar songs gender-inclusive. Children enjoyed changing pronouns. They would decide if they would sing, "The bear went over the mountain to see what he could see" or "what she could see." The Farmer in the Dell might take a "mate" instead of a "wife." This kind of activity provided children with experience and confidence to criticize and change cultural expressions and values. One teacher early in the year introduced the following:

> Bah, bah black sheep,
> Have you any wool?
> Yes, sir; yes, ma'am,
> Three bags full.
> One for my master,
> One for my dame,
> One for the boy and girl (instead of: One for the little boy)
> Who live(s) down the lane.

The teacher sensed that the children were both curious about and resentful of the changes he had made. The resentment seemed to come from their not having been involved in the decision-making process to change the song. They had not been asked if they wanted to change it or how. When asked if they wanted to make any changes or return the song to its original words, some suggested replacing "three bags full" with "four bags full" and adding another line so that a whole bag could be given "to the little boy who lived down the lane" and "to the little girl who lived down the lane." At another time some children wanted to insert "six bags full" into the song with the additional recipients being "the old man who lives down the lane" and "the old woman who lives down the lane." This teacher had inadvertently provided for the simultaneous development of social critique, composition, quantification, and autonomy.

We also realized we needed to help children develop critical skills in reading books. Instead of carefully selecting and allowing only books that were gender and race inclusive, we introduced and discussed with children those that were not. For example, after discussions with the children, a favorite book, *I'm the King of the Castle,* was usually read twice—once with the main character, Teddy Bear, as the king of the castle, and once with the Teddy Bear as the queen of the castle. When we turned to books about Native Americans, however, we were stymied. Available children's books portrayed Native Americans stereotypically dressed in feathers, loincloths, and buckskin and engaged in riding horses, fighting, and dancing with tomahawk in hand. We could not find books in which Native American children were shown doing what they do today.[26] We could not expect our children to see what was missing from these books without some concrete illustrations or evidence. We also knew that we had to resist our temptation to preach or impose our views about the injustices suffered by Native Americans. Many of us felt passionately about this social issue, but we knew that the children should not be expected or persuaded to mirror our feelings and ideas; instead, they needed the tools and opportunity to develop their own. To offset the predominant images in children's books, we asked parents to hunt through magazines to find pictures of current-day Native American children engaged in daily tasks. One photograph was finally found of a Zuni boy brushing his teeth and wearing a shirt and pants not unlike those worn by the children in our school. The photo was large, clear, colorful, and worked beautifully to bring another person into our classroom along with the other illustrations on our walls. Later on, one of the teachers invited one of her friends, a Native American man, to visit our classroom—not to talk or "teach" about being Native American, but simply to eat, play, sing, and tell stories with us as our many other guests did. We relied on the children to ask this "new person" their own questions as they interacted with him. And as they asked him their usual questions, "Where do you live? Do you have kids? How old are they? Do you have a dog? What do you watch on TV? What do you like to eat?" they came to know and like him and invited him to come back—and to bring his kids with him next time.

Chapter 3

Examining Preconceptions

During the three years I was writing my doctoral dissertation, I was also an instructor and the Protestant chaplain at a small Roman Catholic college. It offered degree programs on campus and at a nearby maximum-security correctional facility, and I taught both on campus and at the correctional facility. The campus population was mostly eighteen- to twenty-two-year-old men and women from white middle-class suburbs in New York, New Jersey, and Connecticut. The all-male prison population was predominantly African-American and Latino men from New York City ranging in age from early twenties to early fifties.

I was attracted to the college's prison program after talking with other instructors who taught in it. Without exception, they said that the students at the correctional facility worked harder and were more serious, eager, engaging, and appreciative of the opportunity to learn than were the students on campus. I welcomed and sought out an alternative to the task of motivating on-campus students whose presence in college seemed to depend more on parental expectations and social privilege than on a clearly felt purpose and desperate need to learn.

TEACHING PRISONERS

My style and method of teaching in both settings was influenced by Paulo Freire's critique of monological "banking education" and his proposed dialogical "problem-posing" education. In banking education the teacher narrates, presents, deposits, and regulates the way the world enters into the student, and the student listens, accepts, and receives the teacher's knowledge. In problem-posing education the teacher helps the student identify his or her main concern, interest, or need, is available as a resource for pursuing an understanding of or solution for that situation, helps the student, and is helped by the student in shaping the world. The teacher teaches and is taught.[1]

In the subheading "Teaching Prisoners," "teaching" serves as both verb and adjective (prisoners who are teaching me and whom I am teaching). It is meant to capture the dual subject-object role that students more readily took on at the correctional facility. There the students were actively invested in and shaped the direction and outcome of classroom discussions, proposed their own agenda, and pressed me to contribute from my life experience. They were not simply objects to be filled with what I could and wanted to teach them, but subjects who taught me and one another. They listened and were listened to, provided and sought answers, received and gave ideas and information. By contrast, students on campus expected to be taught and were much more concerned with what I wanted them to learn. On campus I was continually trying to find ways to "light fires under students," while at the prison I was forever wondering what new fire would next be lighted under me.

In both settings I identified openly as a gay man—not as a point of departure, but as a bit of personal information to encourage, or perhaps to permit, students to take their own concerns seriously. On campus, students tended to receive this information without much spoken comment. Remarks were more forthcoming in "anonymous written feedback," a technique that I used with success in courses on campus. Their solicited and protected responses varied from mild shock and disgust to benign acceptance, but their general tendency was to work toward meeting what they thought was my standard of social tolerance. I had to find ways to enable them to be more genuine, forthcoming, and autonomous.

For the inmates, whose daily lives were locked into limitations and repetitive schedules and tasks, class time was seen as an opportunity to challenge and engage one another and the teacher, to speak up and give one's opinion, to think and not be told what to do. There was, to be sure, some fascination and admiration for my being openly gay in an environment which typically discouraged such disclosure. But the initial "reception" or "deposit" of this information was almost incidental to its use as a resource for wider discussion. For example, in a course on Religion and Contemporary Moral Life we were discussing the role of claiming one's tradition as part of developing a moral position. I was pressed by the students to explain what tradition I claimed as a gay man. Well, I had not thought much about it and offered a rather weak dismissal of tradition as a resource for moral formation by gay men. But my students would not have it; and by the end of the semester I had worked through that problem and understood better what my tradition was.[2] They were not putting me on the spot to embarrass me or to "get the teacher." Rather, they were engaging me in a process that would facilitate their own process of reclaiming and examining their respective traditions. Whether or not they approved of my being gay was not at issue here. How I reflected on and processed my personal experience was. They used my way of coming to terms with my experience as a resource for learning how to come to terms with their own experience, and in doing so they assertively nudged me to learn something about myself and them.

CONNECTED AND ENGAGED

I shall digress for a moment here to describe the context and experience of my first coming out in the prison setting. During the orientation of new teachers by prison officials, we were advised not to engage the inmates in personal discussions or to reveal anything about our personal lives. Homosexuality was an especially sensitive and forbidden topic. The residents, we were told, would use their knowledge of such personal details to "con," "kid," or befriend us, to manipulate favors in grading and assignments. Prison is a setting in which such manipulation is practiced, perfected, and often necessary for survival and the few privileges that are granted. I respected the advice I had been given, but I was engaged in teaching courses in religious ethics in which one's personal experience was a beginning point for examining, understanding, and claiming life's meaning. I was requiring discussion and written descriptions of personal experience, but not giving any of my own. Students were holding back—and rightfully so. Their setting was one in which such candid expression was not rewarded, but stigmatized. I had done nothing concrete to normalize or protect what I was requiring from them.

After several weeks of their resistance and my frustration, I told them I needed to have a truthful conversation. I was careful to frame my comments about being gay in utmost seriousness, and they were quick to respond with the wonderfully humorous and affirmative gay street vernacular, "Honey, you're not telling us anything we don't already know!" So much for the power and value of discretion and "passing"! What followed were not questions about the rightness or wrongness of my sexual orientation, but questions about holding a job, making a family, keeping relationships, and dealing with AIDS as a gay man. These questions led to stories about their own cousins, siblings, and friends who were gay.

While I respect and understand the warning and advice that we instructors received in our orientation by the facility, I must also say that teachers were spared much of the day-to-day interpersonal dynamics that typified daily life within the facility. We were a valued measure of relief for prisoners, a resource which provided some distance from and the opportunity to reflect on the everyday. After my coming out to them, students felt compelled to "stand by me," to respect my honesty and "toughness," and to rely on me to receive, respect, and protect their own honesty in papers. When one of the junior administrators of the program sought to remove me because of his fundamentalist Christian opposition to homosexuality, the inmates who worked in the office convinced the senior administrators that I should stay. Several students also came out to me in their personal papers. A bond was formed that did not necessarily signal agreement and similarity, but trust, forthright engagement, and meaningful dialogue. Fundamentalist Muslim and Christian inmates who felt opposed to homosexuality were as likely to respect me, but to speak with their own voices.

The engaging, dialogical, confrontational format of the classroom in the correctional facility was born out of the instructors' willingness to present new ideas with genuine interest in the students' understanding, application, and expansion of those ideas. The test of that willingness for students was the evidence in the classroom of the instructor's own commitment to that same kind of use of ideas in her or his own life. I have never felt more genuinely engaged and accepted as a gay man than I was by the students in prison.

SIDDHARTHA *VERSUS* CEREMONY

The passive-receptive response of students on campus versus the engaging-confrontational response of students in prison is illustrated further by the reading lists I designed for the two settings. On campus, students registered their interest or approval of reading material by doing or not doing the reading. If the readings were classics such as Plato, students tended not to read them or, if they did, not to criticize them. They accepted them and what I had to say about them but found them too difficult to read and comprehend on their own. I made gradual changes over several semesters by trying an assortment of material and gauging their response by their participation in class discussions and their writing in papers. I also provided the opportunity for them to evaluate and rank reading material anonymously in the middle and at the end of each semester. These evaluations were helpful in showing me what was challenging, enjoyable, and helpful for students. I found that audiovisual material from popular culture and experiential more than theoretical literature provided the best catalyst and substance for students' engagement and discussion. Literature that described personal experiences appealed to them, and if I could illustrate and tie in the more difficult theoretical literature with clips from popular television shows, I had their enthusiastic attention and participation.

On the first day of my first course in the correctional facility, however, students challenged me immediately on my proposed reading list. Although I had attempted to make it representative in terms of race, ethnicity, and gender, it lacked the specific particularity that would include and engage them. My "deposit" of what I thought was representative was quite different from what actually represented the backgrounds from which they came and the situations with which they were dealing. Instead of having engaged in a process of working out the reading list with them, I had assumed the role of an outside expert who already knew their needs and could predetermine what they should and would read without consulting with them. Before the next class, I came back with a range of new materials and we negotiated a different set of readings for the semester.

The following example may help to explain the different approaches and successes in each setting. On campus, after several attempts at presenting a text that was accessible, interesting, and personally challenging, I finally found that Hermann Hesse's *Siddhartha*[3] worked well. In addition to its being an easy read, students identified with the difficult choices that Siddhartha made, especially his separation from his parents. His encounters with teachers, romance, and business and the novel's resolution in simple satisfying work let them discuss and examine their own fears and hopes. When I tried to use this same text in the prison setting, students had little interest and rejected it as too tame, easy, and idealistic. That it did indeed speak better to the concerns of those who could afford even to consider the option of giving up privilege and to control their daily movements into and out of society soon became apparent to me. I was compelled to find and use instead Leslie Marmon Silko's *Ceremony*,[4] with its grittier portrayal of a Native American man's life as affected by race, class, and poverty and without the linear and progressive movement toward peaceful and final resolution.

However, including works that were written by people of color did not and was not meant to produce consensus and agreement, but to present issues in ways that bore most directly on the inmates' lives and opened up debate. Some of the most heated discussion occurred when students challenged the work of the African-American theologian James Cone for remaining too tied to and restricted by the academy and Frantz Fanon's *Black Skin, White Masks*[5] for rejecting the invocation of a mythical African past in the struggle for black liberation.

Within the prison setting, little interest was shown in audiovisual materials. Exposed to an ever-present television in their common areas, inmates came to class to struggle with ideas and engage in stimulating conversation. They selected a balance of experiential and theoretical writings, with a leaning toward difficult and provocative theory. I also felt comfortable using books that I had not thoroughly read and evaluated, because students were not as interested in what I had to say about a work as much as they were in grappling with its good and bad points. A book that failed to work or that provoked controversy or disapproval proved as valuable for gaining insight and perspective as those that did not. Students on campus, on the other hand, were less interested in engaging in this evaluative process themselves. They wanted more to be told what were the right books to read, even if they did not end up reading them.

I may seem to be describing a dichotomy here and favoring or prescribing one setting over the other. I do not mean to. Finding that which engages students in any setting is the important task of Freire's pedagogy. If it is audiovisual material from popular culture in one place and hard-edged political theory in another, the point is not to judge it out of context, but its success or failure to encourage inquiry and, in Freire's terms, to facilitate the process of becoming more fully human. A teacher should respond to the particular needs of those within any setting and help them to recognize and pose their own problems.

On campus I had to do some "hand-holding" and to set up a clearer structure for students to engage in active inquiry and to feel confident in doing so. Since examining preconceptions is basic to intellectual inquiry I developed what I came to call an "interdisciplinary model" for examining preconceptions. I chose to examine homosexuality because I had learned from conversations from the resident advisors in the dormitories that the students had strongly felt, unexamined opinions about it. I decided to use an "interdisciplinary" approach to open the possibilities for different ways of thinking about the issues. I shall use the present tense to describe the model as I used it in class.

SURFACING PRECONCEPTIONS

As an introductory exercise for the first class period, I distribute index cards and ask students to write one reason for disapproving of homosexuality and one reason for approving of it. I encourage students to give honest, first-impression responses. I ask for no names on the cards and guarantee anonymity. I also encourage students to try to give reasons for both disapproving and approving, but not to force a reason for either if they do not have one. I have told them that the cards will be collected and given to a student who has volunteered to read them aloud and who will then tear them up. After the reading, as a class, we discuss the responses and make a list of those that are most common. The disapproval list typically consists of "because homosexuality is disgusting, unnatural, abnormal, against my religion, spreads AIDS, and/or because homosexuals seduce children."

The same is then done with reasons for approval. There are significantly fewer entries on the cards, and the predominant ones have to do with freedom of choice, privacy, and civil rights.

A discussion follows that can focus on any or all of the reasons having to do with disgust, abnormality, or unnaturalness. I ask the following kinds of questions to prompt discussion: What makes anything disgusting? How much does not being familiar with something make it disgusting? Can feelings of disgust be gotten over for the sake of doing something that has to be done? For example, if a baby's dirty diaper disgusts a new parent, can she or he get over the disgust so that they repeatedly change diapers without encountering major problems each time? Or, can and should we get over feeling disgusted or repelled by a particular physical disability so we can then get to know people who have it? Is disgust sometimes a signal to avoid something that is dangerous or evil, such as our disgust when we hear about or see torture or genocide? Are there examples of things that used to disgust you and no longer do? Why not? What happened to alter or remove the disgust? How would you respond to lesbians and gay men if they were to say that heterosexuality is disgusting?

Similar kinds of questions can prompt a discussion of other reasons written on the cards. How do we know what is natural or unnatural? Is it something that we learn from what we have been told, from what we observe in nature, or from what we observe in society, in our neighborhood, in our families? Does "natural" mean the way things are in nature or the ways things are supposed to be as determined by a particular group? How can you determine who is right when one person says something is unnatural and another says it is natural? Is procreation more natural than feelings of body pleasure? How would you respond to lesbians and gay men who say that their attraction to members of their own sex is natural to them and not something that they force?

Difference and Disapproval

Questions about unnaturalness or abnormality surface issues about difference and why difference is or is not a reason for disapproval.

What is threatening about someone's not being like you or your not being like them? Can you recall examples of people who were harmful to you because they were different? Can you recall examples of people who were helpful to you because they were different? Do we feel pressure to hide or share our own differences—whether they be feelings, interests, talents, preferences, or physical characteristics? Would you benefit more from living in a homogeneous or heterogeneous society?

These questions and discussions are intended to provide a feel for the difficulty or limitations of thinking from within a single context and imposing thoughts from that context onto situations and people outside of it or different within it.

This first day's discussion needs to close, however, with a consideration of the reasons for approving of homosexuality as well. So-called "positive" as well as "negative" preconceptions need to be examined. The point of the discussion is not that some preconceptions are better than others, but that all preconceptions need to be examined if we are to make and be responsible for our own decisions. For the preconceptions supporting approval of homosexuality, I remind students that the popularization of choice, privacy, and equal rights is recent and normative within a limited context. Not all countries grant them or assume they are inalienable. The discussion concludes, therefore, with asking what limits, if any, would students place on choice, privacy, or rights? From your own experience, why do they think people should have rights? What is the personal advantage or disadvantage in a society that protects rights? Do adolescents have them? When are rights dangerous? And here AIDS and influencing children usually enter the discussion, and the need for clear facts about these issues is underscored. What do we do when facts contradict our own feelings and experience? On the second day I turn to the social sciences—anthropology, psychology, and sociology—to discuss fact-finding and analysis.

Beyond Personal Experience

I distribute three one-page photocopies in class. One is from Margaret Mead's cross-cultural anthropological study *Male and Female;*[6] another is from Sigmund Freud's *Outline of Psycho-Analysis;*[7] the third is from Alfred Kinsey, Wardell Pomeroy, and Clyde Martin's *Sexual Behavior in the Human Male.*[8] These are short enough to be read in class and then discussed. Our previous day's discussion has anticipated much of the issues that will be raised.

I begin with Mead's because I have found that students are curious about cross-cultural comparisons and because the "unnaturalness" that students often ascribe to homosexuality rests on their understanding of masculinity and femininity, which is the subject of Mead's study.

As stated by Mead, our purpose in looking at other cultures is to find variations in human behavior that we might not otherwise be able to imagine as possibilities. Mead's research shows that across cultures ideals of masculinity and femininity vary. A violent man may be the ideal in one culture, but not trusted to head a family in another. But she also shows that within each culture most people fall in the middle or between the culture's ideals of masculinity and femininity. Students remark that they do not look like the fashion models, movie stars, and athletes whom they hold up as ideals, and even the models and stars do not look like their made-up and touched-up photo images.

I find that for eighteen-year-old college students this discussion is personally felt and may be both threatening and a relief. Clothes, body, and physical image are important, and concerns about them do not go away simply because we understand that such norms are culturally relative and that we are pressured to conform to them. So, I do not require or encourage personal remarks from students, and such remarks usually are not forthcoming.

Although I use Mead to discuss femininity and masculinity, I also mention findings from her work and that of other anthropologists showing that homosexual persons are variously regarded across cultures—from being scorned to being tolerated, accepted, or regarded as special and gifted.

While I use cross-cultural anthropology as part of the model for examining preconceptions, the cited facts are not as useful as the underlying methodology. The discussion concludes with the realization that one must be "cross-situational" in examining preconceptions; that is, that some people are raised in families to approve and others to disapprove of homosexuality; that some states have laws against homosexuality, while others do not, and some go so far as to protect lesbian/gay rights; that some religious denominations condemn homosexuality while others accept and welcome lesbians and gay men; that some countries execute lesbians and gay men, while others tolerate or accept them as citizens, with one country even recognizing same-gender marriage. Before deciding whether or not the preconceptions about homosexuality that come out of one's own situation are those that one wants to hold on to, one might want to explore and compare other situations.

Limits of the Prevailing Norm

We next read and discuss the excerpt from Freud's work. The disparity between cultural ideal and actual behavior, appearance, or preference observed by Mead is reinforced by Freud's observations that "certain facts do not fit into the narrow framework" or "the prevailing view" that "human sexual life consists essentially in an endeavor to bring one's own genitals into contact with those of the opposite sex." Freud introduces what he calls "three neglected facts" that "contradict popular opinions on sexuality": (1) sexual activity begins before puberty; (2) genital intercourse may be a part of sexual activity, but not necessarily its focus, totality, or even a part of it for many; and (3) sexual life includes the function of obtaining body pleasure from various zones of the body, a function that subsequently may be brought into the service of reproduction.

Based on the stories and confidences of patients, Freud's observations reveal the limits of the prevailing heterosexual, procreative norm. His findings also normalize and embrace a range and variety of so-called "deviant" feelings and experiences that most or many of us have. We may not fit the very norm against which we measure and subsequently reject lesbians, gay men, or homosexuality.

I find that similarity with and empathy for nonnormative sexuality are prompted by Freud's observation that for many people kissing, touching, looking, caressing, fondling, hugging, and holding are primarily important and enjoyable. There is a strong measure of relief in knowing that these personally felt precious acts are rendered as "accessory phenomena," "introductory acts," or "foreplay" by neither a majority nor by nature, but by a cultural or prevailing view of sexuality as only genital intercourse.

The use and application of the discipline of psychology—at least Freud's approach to it—to examine preconceptions is not limited, however, to these facts about human sexuality. The discipline's recognition that one needs to own, process, and come to terms with one's feelings and the discipline's proposed method for doing so—the confidential therapy session—are even more commanding than these facts. Preconceptions are often maintained by hiding personal feelings and/or pretending that we do not have them, especially when they run counter to a popular view. Preconceptions are often maintained at the expense of what we feel and at the expense of others' not knowing that others feel as we do. These feelings, of course, are not limited to sexuality and affection. Feelings about politics and social issues may be difficult to express, especially among those who may not approve of them.

The Classroom: Not a Place for Confidentiality

To examine preconceptions we must take seriously these feelings, whatever they may be. To pretend that we are not homophobic, sexist, or racist does no good, if we have those feelings. What is important is our willingness to acknowledge whatever our feelings are and to find a safe context in which we can own and discuss those feelings without fear of judgment or penalty. I do not think that the classroom is a confidential context in which such a processing of feelings can occur. Among fellow students whom one does or does not know and before a teacher who has grade-giving power, students wisely, I think, choose for the most part not to be open about feelings, especially unpopular ones. For example, rarely, if ever, would a student express in a class discussion racist or anti-Semitic feelings, and yet conversations I have had with resident advisors confirm that students certainly have those feelings.

The exercise with which I started our discussion of homosexuality, because it protected anonymity, produced responses which would not have been as forthcoming if solicited in an open class discussion, especially one led by an openly identified gay teacher such as myself. But these kinds of exercises are often only indicators of what one needs to discuss and do not necessarily substitute for the discussions themselves. The point is to encourage students to create or find those contexts in which feelings can be freely surfaced and discussed, whether that be with professionals on campus such as counselors, chaplains, and coaches or with support groups, mentors, or friends. The context needs to be one in which feelings are not simply validated and affirmed, but examined and challenged. Although the classroom is not such a confidential context, it may be the place in which a student may recognize her or his feelings and then go on to find where and with whom to discuss them.

Statistics and Quantitative Data

Next, we review and discuss a page of Kinsey's data on the frequency and occurrence of male homosexuality. His statistic that 37 percent, or two out of five males, have at least some overt homosexual experience is usually very surprising. Kinsey's findings that homosexual activity is found anywhere and everywhere challenge the popular understanding that homosexual activity is restricted to a few unusual people in isolated areas in urban settings. Homosexuality is statistically far from being irregular or infrequent, and these findings foster a discussion in which preconceptions about its being unusual, odd, infrequent, or abnormal are reexamined.

In our discussion of Kinsey's data, as in our discussion of Mead's and Freud's work, the specific facts they found out about homosexuality are a take-off point to discuss methods for examining preconceptions, and here the method we identify is the use of systematically collected and analyzed empirical data, from which we can make cautious generalizations. I note that the initial and continuing influence of Kinsey's findings and the reason they must be taken seriously rests on the thoroughness and detail of his questioning technique and on the size and demographic diversity of his sample. The limits are also discussed. These include the all-white male makeup of the sample and the reliance on social institutions as sites from which subjects were drawn. One should not, therefore, generalize his findings to parts of the population not represented in his sample. We close this discussion by imagining and volunteering examples of surveys in which a selective versus a representative sample is more or less advantageous. For example, surveying only white, middle-class men in a survey about poverty would leave out those most affected by it; or a survey about current college life should be selective by focusing on college students, but should be representative in surveying students at a variety of colleges.

Storytelling, Personal Anecdotes, Qualitative Data

The next step in examining preconceptions moves to folklore and popular wisdom. I ask students to remember those songs and stories that were told and read to them as children and that taught or emphasized a particular moral lesson. Common examples are the lesson about hard work and determination in *The Little Engine That Could,* the lesson of slow and steady wins the race in *The Tortoise and the Hare,* and the lesson about personal appearance and social disapproval in *The Ugly Duckling.*

I suggest that these moral lessons within our own folklore often contradict and challenge our preconceptions, that popular wisdom often challenges popular opinion, and that we have a set of standards against which we may examine our preconceptions. I suggest that we consider the story of *Beauty and the Beast,* because it is very well known in our culture. Finding a popular folk story recast in modern cultural trappings on television is not difficult. We watch a clip from the 1980s *Beauty and the Beast* TV series in which the moral of the story is presented, and in the discussion that follows I ask students to state what the moral is. It comes when the troubled young woman's best friend tells her that doing and having what other people do and have is not as important as following your own heart and having friends who will love, support, and not abandon you for doing it.

Students identify with the situation of the young woman—either from being in or from having friends who have been in the situation of dating someone who was not accepted by friends or parents. But also by this time in the course students have been reading and have nearly completed Aaron Fricke's autobiographical book *Reflections of a Rock Lobster: Growing Up Gay in America.*[9] Fricke provides a personal story about coming to terms with being gay in high school. In a way that asks for neither praise nor pity and in terms with which teenagers can identify, he describes loneliness and rejection, the pressure to conform, and the fear of being left out.

Judging from conversations I overhear in hallways and from markings I see on book covers, I would say that many students begin reading it with some resistance and protest. They usually finish by recognizing and claiming Aaron as a peer. His book identifies that which is common to people his age—whether or not they are gay. Students often respond to his story as the friend does to the troubled woman in *Beauty and the Beast.* They respond to his struggle to pursue a same-gender affectional relationship because they know what it means to them to want to have their own relationships taken seriously.

The final step for examining preconceptions focuses on Fricke's book and considers the usefulness of anecdotal data, personal stories, and autobiographical statements. I make the distinction between statistical/quantitative data and anecdotal/qualitative data. Generally speaking, statistics allow for certain kinds of generalizations, while anecdotal data do not. Anecdotal data are illustrative, often touching us and inspiring empathy and compassion. They provide us with insights into the human condition and sometimes prompt us to reflect more profoundly on our own situation. Aaron Fricke lets us see into the life of one gay man and we may gain some understanding about what it means to be gay, but we cannot conclude that he speaks for all gay people or that his situation is like that of all lesbians and gay men. I suggest that sometimes the most interesting stories are those by ordinary, unknown people. Aaron's story is not interesting because he is famous, but because of how he tells his story and what he says. Because ordinary people usually do not think their lives are worth talking about, we must take the initiative and go after them. Social scientists, journalists, and others seek out and interview people to gather information that adds to our understanding of human life.

I make available copies of two interviews and ask students to read them. Both are very short and can be read quickly in class. I have chosen them not only for the clarity and depth of their anecdotal details, but also because the people interviewed differ from Aaron Fricke. Unlike Aaron who is a white, middle-class, high school student from Rhode Island, one of the interviewees is a ninety-year-old, African-American, middle-class lesbian from Detroit. The other interview is with an African-American college student and her bisexual father who is a recovering addict and public health advocate; both live in Washington, DC.[10] Students are eager to say what does or does not make these interviews interesting and informative.

I ask how many students have ever talked to a lesbian or gay man, and at this point in the discussion of homosexuality they do not hesitate to volunteer their own anecdotes about their uncles, aunts, cousins, acquaintances, and siblings. Most do know someone who is gay, and their comments reveal a variety of gay people with a range of different and similar experiences. By uncovering and sharing this information, we are able to take advantage of one of the benefits of working with anecdotal data. Unlike statistics, these data do not allow us to generalize, but they do encourage us to make comparisons and connections and to pose further questions and seek more information. I ask students to think of questions that they would like to ask if they were to conduct formal interviews with gay people. What questions are still unanswered for them?

As a final exercise, I conduct a brief interview exercise with the students as subjects. I distribute index cards and ask students to write a short paragraph—again without their names—in response to any of these questions: What's the most important thing you learned about yourself from Fricke's book or the interview you read? What in the book or interviews did you find helpful in challenging your preconceptions? Why was the book or interviews not helpful in challenging your preconceptions about homosexuality? What specifically challenged your preconceptions and made you think or feel differently? What important differences or similarities do you feel you have with Aaron Fricke or the people interviewed? What do you approve and disapprove of in how these people lived their lives and how others responded to them? The cards are collected and shuffled as before; but instead of one volunteer reading all of the cards, a student suggests that they be passed around so that each can person take one and read it aloud. The closing exercise, then, has each student reading aloud what another student has written on a card.

By using various academic disciplines and approaches, we may have come to realize that to examine preconceptions we need to consider issues from various viewpoints or cross-situationally; we need to be honest about our feelings and willing to come to terms with them; we cannot ignore facts that contradict our preconceptions; we should reflect on and apply standards that we subscribe to, but sometimes forget, neglect, or apply selectively; and we need to listen to the personal experiences of others and take them as seriously as our own.

PRACTICING WHAT I TEACH

My own preconceptions were challenged by my experiences at this small Roman Catholic college. As a doctoral student finishing his dissertation at one of the most progressive and liberal Protestant seminaries in the country, I began teaching here with a bit of trepidation. But even though the college is neither a liberal nor an intellectual stronghold, I was comfortable teaching there as an openly gay man. The students may not have had the polish to soften their language and to avoid the use of stereotypes as would their counterparts in more elite academic settings, but I usually felt that what I got from them was genuine. When they worked through a question or problem, they did so without pretense. One time when I was walking across campus, one of my students yelled from the midst of a group of his friends, "Comstock is a faggot," and then ducked through his dorm door. Seeing who he was, I asked to speak with him the next time I saw him on campus. Without scolding or punishing him, I explained to him how I had felt singled out and ridiculed. He understood, apologized, and became a student who worked hard and who I enjoyed having in my class.

Before beginning to teach, however, I could have used some of my own prescribed methods for examining my preconceptions. For example, empirical studies show that among major Christian groupings, Roman Catholics most often report support for gay civil rights (75 percent), followed by mainline Protestants (72 percent), black Protestants (71 percent), and evangelical Protestants (55 percent).[11] Of these groupings, Catholics also report least often that their clergy speak against homosexuality, least often that they approve of their clergy doing so, and most often that they approve of same-sex marriage.[12] I knew, too, that major breakthroughs in gay religious studies had been accomplished by such Catholic scholars as John J. McNeill,[13] John Boswell,[14] and Charles Curran[15] and that such Catholic leaders as Seattle Archbishop Raymond Hunthausen had reached out to and welcomed lesbians and gay men, often with the result of recrimination by the Vatican. The discrepancy between antigay positions taken by the Vatican and progay positions of American Catholics was apparent then and would reach a high point of clarity in a pastoral letter by the National Conference of Catholic Bishops that advises parents to put love and support for their gay children before church doctrine that condemns homosexual activity.[16]

However, the willingness of many Catholics to support lesbians and gay men—even more enthusiastically than many in my own liberal Protestant denomination—became most apparent to me in my own personal experience. Previous to my doctoral work, I had received the master's degree required for ordained ministry. In addition to that degree, my denomination also requires that to be ordained one must be employed in a ministry position. Even though my denomination encourages its local congregations and agencies to hire lesbian and gay clergy, those that do are rare. Most refuse even to consider the possibility. My own efforts to secure such employment before and during my doctoral studies had met with the usual rejection.

After I started teaching at the college, I approached the director of campus ministry to offer my assistance as a volunteer. This Catholic nun welcomed my offer—as well as my sexual orientation—and created a new position in which I would be the chaplain for the small number of Protestant students on campus. She also included me in planning events with her and other staff members, such as Holocaust Observation Week, Black History Month, and New-Student Orientation. I became an integral and valued member of the ministry team. She encouraged Catholic students to attend my Sunday afternoon services and my luncheon discussion series, and I got to know many Catholic and non-Catholic students through my work as Protestant chaplain. Without being asked, she managed to eke out from her already strained budget a small stipend for my position; and by doing so she let me satisfy the remaining requirement I needed for ordination, employment as a clergyperson.

I soon initiated and followed through with my denomination's ordination process and was ordained that year in New York City. The irony was that my ordination within my own reputedly progay denomination was made possible by a Roman Catholic nun. I asked her to speak at my ordination service; and I was touched that several of my colleagues—both teachers and ministry staff—attended. But what moved me most was that a carload of Catholic students drove down from the upstate campus to attend and celebrate the service with me.

MOVING ON TO OTHER CONTEXTS

I am now an openly gay chaplain and sociology professor at a small liberal arts university. College guide books give it their highest rating for academic standards, admissions selectivity, and ethnic/racial diversity. They also describe the university as progressive, innovative, creative, alternative, intellectual, politically active, and artistic. It is one of a few colleges and universities that publicly welcomes gay students.[17] On campus, sexuality is a much-discussed topic in and out of courses.

I try to relate to students as producers of knowledge, not only as receivers of knowledge, and I think of teaching as a process by which I learn and change, not as a performance in which I try to impress students with my real or imagined brilliance, knowledge, and style. I am not alone in this approach. For example, reflecting on her twenty-five years of college teaching, Jane Tompkins writes that she "had been putting on a performance whose true goal was not to help the students learn but to" make them "have a good opinion of me." She decided, therefore, "to remove myself from center stage" and "to pay more attention to them and less to myself." As Tompkins has done, I, too, lecture less and give students responsibility for preparing and presenting material to the class. For a course that meets twice a week, I usually lead the first meeting and ask students to lead the second meeting. They work in small groups and I meet with each group beforehand to discuss their ideas and strategies, but ultimately they are left on their own. As Tompkins reports, I, too, have found that students have more to say, more of them talk, they talk more to one another than to or for me, and they get more deeply into the material than if I were telling them about it. I do not worry that they do not make the same point that I would make, because they make other, often better, points.[18]

To facilitate discussions in my classes I try to ease the conventional role of the teacher as the one who singularly sets the agenda and instead encourage honesty, provide protection, and promote tolerance.

The exercise I developed at my previous school whereby each student writes a response on an index card and then reads aloud another person's response is one that I continue to use in this setting. But here, as the following example shows, the technique has become more than the teacher's tool and has been taken up, used, and shaped by the students.

In my introductory sociology class, a small group of students was responsible for leading a discussion about Martin Weinberg, Colin Williams, and Douglas Pryor's sociological study *Dual Attraction: Understanding Bisexuality*.[19] They organized the discussion around sexual preference and as an "ice-breaker" exercise asked people to write down what they considered to be their own primary sexual desire or fantasy. A few of the responses were a bit humorous and raunchy. They made people smile and alleviated what might have otherwise been an exercise that was too intense and serious. One person, for example, wanted a chocolate-covered back to lick. But as the cards were read one after the other, a pattern became clear. Most people had written that they wanted to be held, hugged, and cuddled. When the last person finished reading the card they had received, another spontaneously said, "Gee, we asked a question about sex, and it seems as though everyone just wants to be hugged!" This observation was not made critically or with disappointment, but with a realization that brought relief and deflated the tension and expectations that often accompany or prevent discussions about sex.

I think this exercise was successful for the following reasons:

1. The question was posed not by me but by the students who had prepared the class session. It came out of their interests and was asked in the language and manner that would elicit a genuine response. For me to have asked for this kind of personal information would have been presumptuous, and if I had, my question probably would have been received with some suspicion and with attention to what were perceived as my expectations. Within this exercise I too was a participant, not a leader. I responded to the question by writing out my own card, I received and read the card of another, and I listened to the other responses, as everyone else did.

2. The format of the exercise was familiar. Because we had used it before, students knew and trusted its provisions for privacy and anonymity, and because there were thirty-five people in the class, one felt safety in numbers. Each response was one among many others and could not be attributed to any particular person.
3. The collected responses to the question were a surprise. People seemed to have expected descriptions of desires and fantasies that were somewhat illicit, spicy, or at least genital. And I do not think that students in this exercise felt pressured to tame down what they really wanted to say. The spicier responses were well-received and students even seemed to have wished there were more of them. This group of students was not prudish and censorial, and the campus is not a politically, sexually, or socially tame environment. Freedom of expression is one of the most sacred values here. Students would not have had problems taking advantage of this exercise to express themselves. Actually, their responses here probably allowed them to speak with an honesty not encouraged by the bravado of dormitory conversations about sex.

Popular opinion of college sexual behavior as somewhat wild, experimental, and involving a lot of genital intercourse would not seem to reflect what college students actually do or want to do. I was reminded of Freud's observation that contrary to the prevailing view of human sexual life as genital and procreative, for many people kissing, holding, hugging, and touching parts of the body other than the genitals are the primary, most desired, and most satisfying of sexual behaviors. And as Freud had found that these "neglected facts . . . contradicted all the popular opinions on sexuality," the responses that were written on the cards and read by the students in my class contradicted popular views of sexual behavior on college campuses.[20] I do not think that a lecture by me would have inspired and provided students with the same interest in and understanding of Freud's findings as their own leading of the discussion did. Because they posed their own question, chose their own method of inquiry, and produced their own knowledge, the lesson, message, or meaning was not delivered to them and received secondhand.

Chapter 4

Interfacing

PARALLELS AND SIMILARITIES

From writing my doctoral dissertation on violence against lesbians and gay men, I learned that perpetrators most often are adolescent males, young men in their teens and early twenties who usually act in the company of their male peers. They are not concentrated within one social class or racial group more than another. They are not more or less likely to be doing well academically or to be participating in sports or other school activities. Personal histories of psychological problems or criminal behavior are rare. Police officers, court officials, counselors, and educators familiar with perpetrators are nearly unanimous in observing that they are "ordinary kids from ordinary backgrounds." Many do not even act out of personally felt hatred or disapproval of gay people. Typically, the boredom of hanging out with nothing to do on a Saturday or summer evening is relieved by the impromptu suggestion, "Let's go out and get some fags." Often surprised by the damage and injury they have caused, a common refrain is, "We weren't trying to hurt anyone; we were just out for some fun." While social disapproval of homosexuality appears to be the permission they need or use to attack gay people, it does not seem to be the personal reason or motive for doing so. Having fun and fitting in are.[1]

In the same year that my book on antigay violence was published, I began my current position as a university chaplain and professor. I moved into a residential neighborhood bordering the university made up of faculty, students, and townspeople. I had been hired as an openly gay man and had been "out" for twenty years. I saw myself in all aspects of my life as a confident, openly gay man. My partner was a professor at a university in the next state, but that year he was on sabbatical and spent most of his time with me. I was sure that the people in the neighborhood simply knew that the two new men were a couple. I got to know people in the neighborhood through casual conversations in passing. One day I was talking with my next-door neighbor, a retired man, about his garden, and he asked me if I was married (and he did not mean to another man). I said, "No," and moved to another topic and quickly ended the conversation. I walked away with my gay pride and virtue deflated. What had happened to the completely open, proud gay man? Why hadn't I said or explained that I was gay? Without a pause and without conscious or deliberate self-hatred or disapproval of homosexuality, I had acquiesced and acted to fit in.

I would appear to have something in common with some perpetrators of antigay violence. On occasion, without thinking carefully and without intending to, we choose to fit in rather than to affirm, stand up for, or recognize the full humanity of gay people. This personal similarity is reinforced by a social one. Neither adolescent males nor gay men have a powerful or secure place within the social order. Antigay violence is perpetrated for the most part by members of one socially insecure group against members of another.

In drawing parallels and similarities between perpetrators and myself, I do not think I have to tell you that personally I feel on uncomfortable ground here. It would be simpler and easier for me to view perpetrators of antigay violence as weird, sick, antisocial malcontents who represent nothing but a fringy brand of hatred. But they are not and they do not. In an anonymous survey that I did of my own students where I formerly taught, 51 percent of the men reported they had verbally harassed gay people and 16 percent reported having physically attacked them. As a former high school teacher and current college chaplain and professor, I work and live in the midst of the population statistically most likely to attack me. To begin the task of recognizing and working with the similarities between us, I shall use three resources to develop a model for "interfacing."

RESOURCES FOR INTERFACING

Gloria Anzaldua uses sewing terms to define "interfacing" as "sewing a piece of material between two pieces of fabric to provide support and stability to collar, cuff, yoke."[2] My resources—my material, fabric, and joinings—are selective, and my bias in making them work together, to provide support and stability for one another, is admitted and intentional. I look not for cause and effect or direct influences between them, but instead I recognize similarity, complement, or possible alliance. I seek to bring together what has not been brought together before as a way to develop a model that I can then use to interface with adolescent men. Two of these resources are drawn from research projects, separate from my dissertation, that I conducted at Union. In one I studied writings by lesbians of color, and in the second I studied cross-cultural anthropology, especially the work of Margaret Mead. The third resource is a recommendation that came later from one of my students. It is the theory of "situated knowledges" developed by science historian Donna Haraway.

I shall first outline and describe lesbian-of-color theory and the opportunity it offers for interfacing with Mead's method.[3] To discuss Mead's work I shall use as my primary resource anthropologist Catherine Bateson's book about her parents, *With a Daughter's Eye: A Memoir of Margaret Mead and Gregory Bateson.*[4] Finally, with the help of Haraway's theory of situated knowledges in her book *Simians, Cyborgs, and Women: The Reinvention of Nature,*[5] I shall apply my interface of lesbian-of-color theory and Mead's method to my own work as a chaplain and sociology professor.

I fashion my interfacing by recognizing the differences between the fabrics I bring together. These include differences in the race, age, historical period, experience, and professional status of the writers. Mead was a white woman who became a well-known anthropologist and a curator at the American Museum of Natural History in New York City before World War II and continued to work and write until her death in 1978. Haraway, also white, is a professor at the University of California, Santa Cruz, whose work gained recognition in the 1980s. The lesbians of color whom I discuss are writers whose work began to appear in the early 1980s. They have taught at the university level but not in full-time, permanent positions. I acknowledge the difficulty and superficiality of simply lining and reinforcing one set of experiences with the other, and I expect instead the different cut, the awkward gathering, and mismatch of cloths brought together to make a collar or a cuff. But it is the African-American lesbian Audre Lorde herself who gives me the permission and encouragement to make this interface:

> We have *all* been programmed to respond to the human differences between us with fear and loathing and to handle that difference in one of three ways: ignore it, and if that is not possible, copy it if we think it dominant, or destroy it if we think it subordinate. But we have no patterns for relating across our human differences as equals. As a result, those differences have been misnamed and misused in the service of separation and confusion.
>
> Certainly there are very real differences between us of race, age, and sex. But it is not those differences between that are separating us. It is rather our refusal to recognize those differences, and to examine the distortions which result from our misnaming them and their effects upon human behavior and expectation.[6] (Printed with permission from *Sister Outsider* by Audre Lorde, copyright 1984. Published by the Crossing Press, Santa Cruz, California).

Lorde's clear and adamant advice "that we not hide behind the mockeries of separations"[7] compels me to make the interface, to *create* the pattern of connection between the work of a white woman and women of color. But I also *find* a connecting point of similarity between Lorde and Mead in Mead's words.

In her *Rap on Race* with James Baldwin, Mead, similar to Lorde, recognized the unavoidable presence and effect of human differences in our social relationships: "It's true, you've got to be taught to *hate,* but the appreciation and fear of difference is everywhere."[8] And she understood as well that our responses to these differences are shaped by dominant social forces. She saw, for example, that her previous position on racism—to ignore race, to ignore difference, to try to be color-blind—became totally unacceptable with the advent of black power and had to be changed: "Saying, 'We'll pretend that you're like us' . . . means of course that 'We'll deny you. . . . We deny you when we accept you; we deny the ways you are not exactly us, by ignoring them.' "9

CENTRAL VIEWPOINT
OF LESBIAN-OF-COLOR THEORY

What sustains my interfacing of lesbian-of-color theory with Mead, however, is not Lorde's permission, but the central viewpoint developed and articulated by her claim that "there is no hierarchy of oppressions." She writes that as a "Black lesbian feminist socialist mother of two, including one boy, and a member of an interracial couple, I usually find myself a part of some group defined as other, deviant, inferior, or just plain wrong,"10 and "I have learned that oppression and the intolerance of difference come in all shapes and sizes and colors" but "arise from the same source," which is "a belief in the inherent superiority of one" of those differences "over all others."11

Other lesbians of color, such as Cherrie Moraga, agree that "the danger lies in ranking the oppressions."12 Their warning is persuasive not because it comes from an abstract notion or "good idea," but because they experience those oppressions simultaneously. Barbara Smith reports that "we examined our own lives and found that everything out there was kicking our behinds—race, class, sex, and homophobia."13 They found that absent the actual and simultaneous experience of these various oppressions others do not have to take them all seriously and fight against all of them.

Lorde says that those who "stand outside the trappings of power often identify one way in which [they] are different" and then "assume that to be the primary cause of all oppression," but "we came to realize that our place was the very house of difference rather than the security of any one particular difference."14 Others can ignore this social complexity because they focus only on the issue bearing most directly on them and then particularize it exclusively or universalize it.

Merle Woo contends, for example, that most of the time when white women claim to be looking for "universal" themes, the term "is just a euphemism for 'white.' "15 Lorde and Smith point out that the tendency within the women's movement is for white women to "focus upon their oppression as women and ignore differences of race, sexual preference, class, and age"[16] and that "many forces in the Black community would have us . . . pretend that sexism, among all the 'isms,' was not happening to us."[17] Moraga observes that poverty and classism tend to be forgotten "in the rising Black middle class" and "among white gay men" because "to remember may mean giving up whatever privileges we have managed to squeeze out of this society by virtue of our gender, race, class, or sexuality."[18]

For lesbians of color, however, such single-issue approaches neglect or undermine other issues that bear directly on their survival and efforts to lead meaningful lives. Woo asserts that "until we can all present ourselves to the world in our completeness, as fully and beautifully as we see ourselves naked in our bedrooms, we are not free."[19] As Smith observes, "our efforts to comprehend the complexity of our situation as it was actually occurring" rendered arguments about the primacy of sexism, racism, classism or homophobia as hollow and inadequate for understanding and changing the social order. She maintains that the "concept of the simultaneity of oppression" is "the crux" and "one of the most significant ideological contributions" of lesbian-of-color theory.[20]

THE OPPORTUNITY FOR INTERFACE

These two observations by lesbians of color, (1) the absence of and need for patterns for relating across differences, and (2) the simultaneity and interaction, rather than hierarchy, of oppressions, signal for me the opportunity for interfacing their work with Mead's.

Catherine Bateson tells us that in 1925 Mead ignored the cautions of her professor Franz Boas and "her father's attempts to constrain her to the ordinary" and left the United States for Samoa to immerse herself in a different cultural system with "the recognition that the difference is orderly." With others, including her husband Gregory Bateson, Mead worked with the understanding developed by anthropologist Ruth Benedict that a culture could be characterized by a single pervasive cultural configuration. But Benedict taught anthropologists to discover in other societies both the ordinary or normal as well as the dissonant, even if it frightened them or made them uncomfortable. Mead, better than others, understood that this common pattern, this expectation of internal homogeneity, led to another important insight, that a culture could incorporate sharply contradictory or contrasting themes, so that anthropologists could think in terms of layers of complex paradox.[21]

Margaret and Gregory, as Catherine Bateson refers to her parents in her book, each saw pattern and regarded details differently. In his later work, she writes, Gregory sought "the pattern that connects all living beings in formal similarities of growth and adaptation" and said that "to see these overarching patterns at all you may have to ignore a tremendous amount of superficial diversity." It did not matter greatly to him whether he studied a group of people, a disease, or animals, "for the same kinds of formal pattern could be discerned in different bodies of data. The proprieties of life, and the details of custom . . . seemed to him increasingly irrelevant." Catherine reports that his interest in abstraction brought him to cybernetics and information theory, two highly abstract and formal areas of theory. "Cybernetics was for him the study of ways in which a system, perhaps one with many parts, can sustain a complex process so that irregularities are corrected for and the system remains within certain parameters."[22] Margaret, on the other hand, perceived and valued differences and accentuated them "as interesting in themselves, rather than as deviations from the ideal." For her, "even those things that may have been accidental or simply assumed were afterward treated as part of the pattern," and her "elaboration of detail" and "wish to specify it exactly were rooted in precise and elaborate fieldwork" studying eight different peoples.[23]

According to Catherine, Gregory "lacked [Margaret's] fascination with pervasive elaboration" and instead was "adept at focusing with brilliant clarity on a single point of high patterning" and "unconcerned by a surround of messiness that was not neatly integrated into the single configuration." When observing cock fights in Bali, for example, he recorded how the men's hands moved to echo the conflict, but was not interested in "the mass of background detail," even of the fighting cocks themselves. Margaret struggled for the particular moment of insight that would lead to a massive effort of documentation and for better and better methods of observing and recording. "Gregory was dissatisfied when the insight was specific to a single culture and strained for a formal framework of description that would be deductive, unto which specific insights could be mapped." Margaret "was reluctant to see any pattern stripped down to basics" and sought instead to introduce greater diversity, to enrich and elaborate rather than to simplify, always to be taking in and using new material.[24]

Catherine says that "much of Margaret's appetite for detail came from a desire to step into other frames of reference," and these ranged from distant cultures to her daughter's school:

> Sometimes Margaret would announce that she wanted to interview me on some issue, and this was a signal that she wanted rich description, not just opinion—a narrative of how such issues as holidays were handled at the Downtown Community School that might explain tension between Jewish and Gentile parents, for instance.[25]

In the same way, Margaret moved around the world, engaged in conversations with as many people as possible, took down what people said, passed them on to other people in other places, and told people to get in touch with others whose work related to their own.[26]

While it may seem that I am heading this comparison of Margaret and Gregory toward asserting that gender-specific behavior or experience of women is preferable over that of men, such is not my intention. Actually, Catherine says that one of their friends told her, "Your mother has such a masculine mind and your father such a feminine mind. . . . Margaret is always shooting thousands of ideas out in all directions, like sperm, while Gregory, when he has an idea, he sits on it and develops it like a big ovum."[27] Probably neither Margaret nor Gregory can be relied on to represent the conventions of their sex or gender. My purpose in comparing them is to highlight and develop the basis for interfacing Mead's work with that of lesbians of color.

A METHOD OF CONNECTION AND INTERACTION

Catherine reports that Mead carried a notepad with her in which she was continually "writing down any new idea or information she thought she might want to use," and she places great importance on the notebook for understanding Mead's method:

> The notebook stands in my mind for a whole way of working whereby she was constantly taking in new material and using, incorporating reactions, so that an interesting piece of work she heard about in Florida would be talked about in Topeka and synthesized with what someone was thinking in Boston, elaborated in Cincinnati, incorporated in a lecture in California.[28]

Mead also instructed her students to write things down when they occurred to them, to "*date* every scrap of paper" and "to hoard the record of [their] inquiries and [their] errors." She emphasized "the importance of recording first impressions and saving those first few pages of notes instead of discarding them in the scorn of later sophistication, for the informed eye has its own blindness as it begins to take for granted things that were initially bizarre."[29]

The notebook, which Catherine claims "stands for [Margaret's] whole way of working," is the thread that joins and tightens the interface of the work of Mead and lesbians of color. Mead's advice to write in and grasp the moment, to eschew standards of sophistication that blind one to seeing the bizarre, is echoed in Anzaldua's advice to women of color to "forget the room of one's own—write in the kitchen, lock yourself up in the bathroom."[30] To be sure, one can say that what Mead offers as advice is an academic or privileged choice, while what Anzaldua offers comes from economic need and survival; but I do not think that the similarity is facile and coincidental. For each moves decidedly from the particular to analysis, from the moment of insight to further documentation, from observation to understanding. Each is inductive.

FUSING EXPERIENCE, THEORY, AND SOCIAL REALITY

Margaret's search for and the elaboration of detail and difference were distinct from Gregory's search for overarching frames of reference and his preferred dismissal of what he considered "superficial diversity," and they seam smoothly with Anzaldua's claim that "no topic is too trivial."[31] This seam of eschewing the universal, abstract, and deductive for the particular, observed, and inductive is further secured by inductive theory's basis in concrete reality. As Anzaldua warns against "not fusing our personal experience and world view with the social reality we live in,"[32] so does Catherine tell us that Margaret urged and helped her students to get out of the academy and into the world. She argued against shaping "anthropological research to fit laboratory models of hypothesis testing" and was "one of the first anthropologists to prepare students for the field in a practical way, teaching them actual techniques."[33]

Like lesbians of color, Mead proposes a method for relating across differences that is based on the surfacing and elaboration of particularity and detail, especially that which has been devalued or disempowered by dominant social forces. But the thread that finally tightens the seam and completes the interface is not simply inductive theory's location in and attachment to concrete reality, but its propensity for advocacy and social change:

> In everything that Margaret wrote she took into account the question of what it would be helpful for people to know and how they might move from concept to concept without distortions that would be damaging. She believed in putting knowledge to work and in both seeking and expressing it in ways that would put it at the service of humankind, while Gregory would move toward the exploration of abstract idea, reaching for an amoral elegance.[34]

Anzaldua claims that theory is "a mental plan of the way to do something" that changes people.[35] Catherine tells us that Margaret, too, "saw the whole of theory making as having social implications." While Gregory would worry about "becoming bogged down in specifics," Margaret worried about how her work "would be helpful, allow better education or better cross-cultural understanding." Margaret worked with the understanding that her research would have "an effect on how people acted" and that she was "thus engaged in social construction."[36]

The test of my interface of Mead's method and lesbian-of-color theory must rest with Mead, for she, unlike lesbians of color, had the academic privilege of removing herself from what Anzaldua calls "the pull between what is and what should be."[37] But Mead's privilege should not be overstated, especially since she made a name for herself before the feminism of the 1970s. Catherine reports that

Mead's role at the Museum of Natural History was "ambiguous" and that she remained an associate curator for many years, "like so many women in academe who were not given appropriate status. She worked around the problems, cannily expanding her work space in the tower where male curators were not interested in competing, raising her own funds, and increasing her freedom to come and go as she liked."[38]

TESTING THE THEORY

Mead does appear to have demonstrated a consistent effort and "desire to step into other frames of references," to put herself in particular situations that would change her. As Catherine tells us, in the numerous conferences she initiated and organized throughout her professional years, she brought together groups of people who replicated "the diversity of the culture under study, who could represent not only the classes of individuals but, in their relationships with each other, the relationships between the sexes or the generations or between different ethnic groups in the population." She was not interested in having "one of each" or in a "statistical kind of representation," but in "being sure that the group reflected certain kinds of relationships, certain inevitable contrasts of approach."[39]

For example, in their *Rap on Race,* Catherine says Mead and James Baldwin "evoked the sense of multiple dyads challenging each other with different kinds of wisdom, a man and a woman, black and white, a poet and an anthropologist." Mead also sought to include people of all ages in her conferences and dialogues. After realizing that her ongoing work involved the same senior scholars and professionals and that younger people were not being included, she "undertook an ongoing battle to get younger people brought into the discussion." Because she assumed there were "real differences in experiences," she sought neither experts on youth nor "someone to act out the role of youth but to embody it." Her efforts "to incorporate even more people into the multilogue" included asking audiences at her public talks to write their questions and comments. She later read through all those to which she did not have time to respond. Gregory, on the other hand, focused on "a small set of highly abstract themes all his life" and tolerated those people who "came and went if they were interested in engaging with his ideas."[40]

Catherine reports that Margaret, therefore, was popular with "ordinary people" because "she affirmed and respected their ways of doing things, their decencies and aspirations, even if she did not herself conform," whereas Gregory was popular with the counterculture. Margaret chose to speak and write for a broad audience that went well beyond the boundaries of academia. Her regular column for *Redbook* magazine demonstrated her interest in and respect for the everyday issues of middle-class women. But she did not pander to convention and the status quo. For example, in one issue she spoke favorably about bisexuality and discussed the lessening of taboos and laws against homosexuality, and her 1949 book *Male and Female: A Study of the Sexes in a Changing World* was a turning point for gaining a cross-cultural perspective on homosexuality and showing that homosexuals were regarded favorably in other cultures.[41]

IMPLICATIONS FOR TEACHING

I seek to recognize and create the interface of lesbian-of-color theory and Mead's anthropological method because academics and scholars have the tendency and privilege to escape or wander from concrete reality and to hierarchize or ignore various kinds of experience when proposing solutions for various social problems. Mead's method of personal observation and participation seems to counter this tendency because it is accompanied and directed by a critique and subversion of social dominance, superiority, and separation. In the academy, deductive approaches (applying abstract theories to selected sets of experiences) prevail over inductive approaches (working from particular experiences to develop a theory).[42] I find that Mead's method avoids the tendency toward abstraction and the devaluing of particularity and experience.

The distinction that I make between "inductive" and "deductive" approaches has recently been made by science historian Donna Haraway as the difference between "embodied" and "disembodied" objectivity. Embodied objectivity, which she advocates, is based on "situated knowledges" or what we know from our experiences within our particular social situations. Disembodied objectivity is based on "transcendent knowledge," or what we know by distancing ourselves from what we study. Haraway is suspicious of the latter approach because it is "an illusion" or "false vision promising transcendence of all limits":

> The only way to find a larger vision is to be somewhere in particular. The science question in feminism is about objectivity as positioned rationality. Its images are not about the products of escape and transcendence of limits, i.e., the view from above, but the joining of partial views and halting voices into a collective subject position that promises a vision of the means of ongoing finite embodiment, of living within limits and contradictions, i.e., of views from somewhere.[43]

By pretending not to be personally interested or invested and by not acknowledging our limits, we do not have to take responsibility for whom or what we study. As Lorde notes:

> When we live outside ourselves, . . . on external directives only rather than from our internal knowledge and needs, . . . then our lives are limited by external and alien forms, and we conform to the needs of a structure that is not based on human need, let alone on an individual's. But when we begin to live from within outward, . . . allowing that power to inform and illuminate our actions upon the world around us, then we begin to be responsible to ourselves in the deepest sense.[44] (Reprinted with permission from *Sister Outsider* by Audre Lorde, copyright 1984. Published by the Crossing Press, Sana Cruz, California.)

Situated knowledge is admittedly only a partial perspective, but one that promises objectivity and clarity not by viewing from a distance but by "connection." Situated knowledges become objective when they are joined and one learns "how to see faithfully from another's point of view."[45]

I see the nonhierarchy and simultaneity of oppressions experienced and theorized by lesbians of color as a prototype for Haraway's embodied objectivity. The connection of different oppressions and experiences within the life of a lesbian of color prescribes and models the connection of experiences among and across people advocated by Haraway. Furthermore, by refusing to claim exclusive rights on any particular form of oppression or experience and by encouraging other people to value and to relate to others across their differences, lesbians of color deflate their own or any others' exclusive or unilateral authority to diminish, dismiss, or abuse particular experiences.

Haraway concedes that a serious danger in diminishing the value of disembodied or transcendent knowledge is romanticizing the situated knowledges of the less powerful. Without an authority from on high telling us what to think, see, and do, we may too easily shift into idolizing any particular experience or person that appeals to us or seems attractive, esoteric, or different.[46] Lorde insists that to relinquish power to a higher authority or to grant power exclusively to a lesser one is to sidestep the more important and difficult project of satisfying our needs "in concert with others" and "to use each other as objects . . . rather than make connections with our similarities and differences."[47] Such connection is not achieved cheaply, but often only through honest expressions of anger, discomfort, and conflict and usually within contexts that promote collaborative and mutual decision-making processes. The test for embodied objectivity must be the relentless, expansive, and endless joining of knowledges from various situations and, as Haraway notes, none is "exempt from critical re-examination, decoding, deconstruction, and interpretation."[48]

The importance, necessity, and difficulty of examining and criticizing both self and others are also illustrated in Catherine's disappointment with and criticism of her mother for not sharing the details of her same-sex relationships:

> I knew little until after her death of the pattern of relationships to male and female lovers that she had developed, so that trying to look back on who she was as a person and as my mother has been complicated by the need to deal with the fact of concealment. I have been at times angered at the sense of being deliberately deceived and at having been without a doubt a collaborator in my own deception, limiting my perceptions to the images she was willing to have me see. I have sometimes felt myself doubly bereaved as well, having radically to reconsider my convictions about who she was and therefore, in relationship to her, about who I was and am, surprised at last by the sense of continuing recognition.[49]

Catherine says she surfaces these personal details about Mead not because "the public belongs in her bedroom," but because "Margaret Mead has walked in a thousand bedrooms, has been a touchstone for parents trying to understand the sexuality and sexual orientation of their children, has helped and hindered women trying to understand themselves and their potential." In retrospect, Catherine requires of Mead the kind of honesty, vulnerability, personal observation, and attention to detail that Mead prescribed for others. Setting forth the same conditions for reciprocity that Haraway also outlines and discusses, Catherine says, "Those who have attended to her words have, I believe, the right to know something of her experience, even as they realize that no one can fully represent in the single life they lead the full human potential of their vision."[50]

As a gay, white, middle-class, male chaplain and sociology professor, finding a way to relate to adolescents as full human beings as I would want them to relate to me is no easy task. As Lorde also observed, "We have no patterns for relating across our human differences as equals." And, of course, she is right. The social patterns available to us militate against relating to adolescents as equals, because society "needs" adolescents to be less than equal to adults. Alternative patterns for relationships need to be made against the grain. To begin the task of recognizing and working with the similarities between us, I first acknowledge Audre Lorde's observation that "there is no hierarchy of oppressions."[51]

Without going into a lot of detail about "adolescence," I do want underscore that it is a socially constructed rather than biologically determined category inserted between childhood and adulthood. And the age range of the category has widened considerably since the beginning of the twentieth century, with the movement from agrarian to industrial and high-tech economies and with the increased human life span. The teenage years and early twenties have become a time of preparation for rather than active participation in society, even though these young people "in terms of physical and mental vitality . . . are at the top of the arch of life." As research by Mihaly Csikszentmihalyi shows, most teenagers feel as though they have been put on hold while their best years drift by, and as a result they report feeling less strong, active, alert, and motivated than other age groups, including senior citizens. They feel their position to be one of "weakness and constraint." Most adults do not want to recognize that young people need "powerful skills," "worthy challenges," and "adventures involving risks." And we do not treat them "as fully formed persons who should have access to meaningful experiences." Desperate attempts by young people to find suitable challenges—sometimes in the form of hurting themselves or hurting others—often do, but should not surprise us.[52]

If we define oppression as preventing a person or people from becoming fully human,[53] the situation for many, if not most, adolescents is oppressive. But while Lorde admonishes us not to rank or hierarchize oppressions, she also does not suggest that we equate them. I am not proposing that adolescents, especially adolescent males, are as oppressed as or more oppressed than other people and groups. Instead, I want to recognize the particularity of their oppression as a way to understand and change a behavior that threatens my life and to learn to understand it with them.

I find the interface of lesbian-of-color theory, Mead's method, and Haraway's theory of situated knowledges helpful for several reasons: one is the shared premise that no experience, situation, or situated knowledge is better than another. Each person is responsible not to argue for the superiority of her, his, or another's situated knowledge, but to examine, criticize, appreciate, and describe it in detail, to acknowledge the partialness of one's view, to understand what one does not know or needs to know, to make it available to others, and to accept, understand, criticize, and appreciate other situated knowledges. Situated knowledges, therefore, are vulnerable in a positive sense to reexamination and change, but also must guard against romanticizing the other or dismissing oneself. Neither teacher or student is a reigning expert above the fray of society nor an uncritical observer of it, but an engaged participant, researcher, and agent in it.

Second, I find Haraway's specific terms helpful. In spite of efforts to clarify, redefine, sharpen, or broaden the term "oppression," I do not find it a useful term in working with students. It is so overused and its meaning is so limited or diffuse as not to provide and provoke engaging discussion. For most students, it is a term that prejudges, signals negativity, and means that we shall be talking about weakness and victimization. "Situated knowledge," on the other hand, invites and requires original participation. It signals to students that they are needed and responsible for filling out their knowledge with particulars known only to them, that the discussion cannot go on without their doing so, and also that the situations of others need to be understood and examined in the complexity and ambiguity of various, similar, and conflicting experiences, not in ready-made categories of dehumanization. Each person, including the professor, has the responsibility to acknowledge her or his own limits and strengths for interacting and connecting with others in and beyond the classroom and to make changes in her or his situation because of new knowledge gained through such interactions and connections.

Third, students have been trained by the academy not to include their personal experience in their work and even to disparage it as a resource for intellectual analysis and growth. Rarely are they asked to write about themselves, to observe their place among and relationships with others, to take Mead's advice to document their observations of themselves, to learn, as Anzaldua did, that "no topic is too trivial," or, to do as Haraway advocates, "to learn in our bodies . . . to name where we are and are not." I have found that straight-identified young men more than others feel their experience counts for nothing, either because as males they have been socialized to think they should rise above personal problems and feelings or because the liberal canon of experiential literature leans toward the "marginalized." Most are unprepared for and surprised that anyone would be interested in their situated knowledge. That an older gay man encourages them to take seriously their own experience as a valuable tool for intellectual inquiry, to describe, examine, and contribute their situated knowledge to wider discussion, is significant and groundbreaking for many. That such a discussion, context, and format allow and encourage me to do the same, to acknowledge and examine my own experience, which may not be unlike their own, testifies, I think, to the connectional opportunities of relating across our differences or to what Haraway calls "the joining of partial views and halting voices into a collective vision."[54]

In my courses students hand in papers in a way that allows me to read each one first "name-blind" and then knowing who wrote it. Such double reading lets me first step back from preconceptions that I may have about the writer and then consider the paper in relation to her or his previous work and what I know about the student. I combine "disembodied" and "embodied" objectivity in this process so that I remain neither a distant, transcendent, cool reader nor one who is too familiar, sympathetic, and warm. The combination helps me avoid the "danger of romanticizing any one situated knowledge" that Haraway warns against and lets me be more open to, surprised and challenged by, and both critical and supportive of each student's writing. When I started using this process for evaluating papers, many times I would read a paper that was intensely personal, emotional, and vulnerable, assume that the writer was a woman, and then discover it was not. I have found that when given encouragement and opportunity, men much more than women choose to write about their personal relationships and to discuss their feelings. Their papers often deflate gender stereotypes—and I was not immune from such stereotypes and having them challenged.

My interactions with male undergraduates have provided me many opportunities to see that we have much in common and much to learn from each other. Although those in their gender-and-age group are statistically the most likely to attack me, I have also found that my male students work seriously to define their masculinity by other than conventional standards, to confront their own and others' homophobia, and to think and act with regard for the humanity of others. In class once, while discussing my research on perpetrators of homophobic violence, I presented this contradiction between my data and my experience. Several students suggested that a future research project should perhaps be a collection of stories about adolescent men who are the antithesis of perpetrators. They were right, of course, and this chapter is a direct result of their suggestion. Although I have not formally collected those stories, I shall include a brief one here.

My partner and I have a friend who is a single mother. About ten years ago, her son was in high school and had a pack of friends who enjoyed pushing the boundaries of acceptable behavior. Their hair, clothes, music, truancy, and attitude often put them at odds with school authorities. As a nonparent, I could often "enjoy" our friend's stories about their acts of rebellion, because I was not directly affected by them. One story, however, has stayed with me more than the others. The usual Saturday night hang-out was at her house, so she overheard some of what was going on and was filled in later by her son. One of his friends was quite nervous, said he had something to say, but fumbled around for awhile before he could finally tell the others that he was gay. He wanted them to know but was afraid that they would reject him. They listened and encouraged him to tell them more. How long he had known? Had he told his parents? Who was he attracted to? Did he have or want a boyfriend? They stayed up all night talking. What they insisted on throughout the night was not only that they accepted him, but they wanted to do whatever they could to make his being gay easier and better. They were his friends and would not abandon him.

As I have listened to young men in my role as a college professor and chaplain I am often amazed at how much more open, sensitive, and mature they are then I was at their age. Their ideas and experiences often surprise me and force me to evaluate my experience, stereotypes, and settled ways of thinking. As a result, my conversations with young men have caused me to rethink my relationships with older straight men; and as I look back on the years spent obtaining my PhD, and getting and staying hired, I realize that the people who not only stood by me but stepped forth to advocate for me have most consistently been straight men.

Expanding the Range of Interfacing

When I began my doctoral studies and needed the requisite advisor, I had trouble finding a faculty member who would work with an openly gay man. The closeted gay faculty seemed terrified of and were even hostile to me; and the women felt that gay issues fell outside of their own academic interest in feminism. A straight white man was the only one who was interested in working with me and he turned out to be a remarkably supportive, steadfast, attentive advisor. When I attempted to get ordained as an openly gay clergyman within my denomination, I was repeatedly rejected by local congregations and then ignored by the denominational leadership and even by the denomination's gay caucus, until two straight white men stepped up to the situation and successfully marshaled me through the process. When I sought my first full-time position after being ordained and receiving my doctoral degree, a straight black man was instrumental in welcoming me and getting me hired as an openly gay college chaplain. When the teaching part of my position as chaplain was in jeopardy because of fiscal constraints, a straight man took the initiative to find other funds.

The realization that straight men have been my main advocates comes as a bit of a jolt because I had rather uncritically considered the gay community and feminist women to be my base of support. But the dynamics and distribution of power within the academy have forced many lesbians and gay men to hide and protect themselves and compelled feminist women to limit and defend their programs. As a result, indifference, silence, avoidance, fear, and obstruction have as often as not been their response to openly gay scholars and clergy.

Some may say that straight men have done the most for me because they have the institutional power and position to do so, but none of the men who have helped me had to do what they did. Their support and actions were not a necessary or expected part of their positions; they gained no additional power or status by doing so; and their efforts required risking their own popularity and credibility within the institutions. Besides, women are not without institutional power within my denomination or the college at which I am employed, and gay people are welcome.

I do not wish to demonize gay men and feminist women nor to divinize straight men. Certainly, the latter have been the cause of some of my closest calls with professional rejection and termination. Nor am I claiming that the support I have received from straight men represents a majoritarian movement. Recent polls showing that the majority of men oppose and the majority of women support gay rights[55] give me pause in becoming optimistic about the readiness of men to relate across our human differences. But these discouraging signs also compel me to take advantage of and encourage what I see as a subsocial pattern of straight men advocating for and supporting gay men.[56] Such advocacy and support do exist and I want to acknowledge my own complicity in not having recognized them fully.

If I am to be honest, I must admit that I have tended to fortify myself with the belief that straight men do not think, feel, or know much, because such bravado compensates for my precarious position within the academy and anticipates or prepares me for discrimination within it. Such defensiveness is not without necessity and merit. Several years ago, for example, a group of conservative Christian male professors tried to have me removed from my chaplaincy position, and they applied nearly enough behind-the-scenes pressure to be successful. Later, when the Dean was leaving for a position at another school, she told that they could not have come any closer to getting their way. For me to focus on their efforts and not to say how other straight men have been my friends and advocates would be to let them have their way and not to make the connections that build and increase inclusive community.

But I am also left with the central amd compelling aspect of inter-facing—to challenge, reassess, reform, and restructure my current relationships, especially those with which I have become too content and comfortable. If interfacing is indeed at the heart of how I want to conduct my work, isn't it necessary for me to find a way to connect to the professors with whom I do not agree? To be sure, such an effort may involve an "awkward gathering and mismatch of cloths," but if it is reinforced with mutual respect and honesty, it should produce a sta-ble collar or cuff.

Chapter 5

Writing for Students

GOD TALK

As a university chaplain I enjoy the challenge of writing for students. In addition to my scholarly publications for an academic audience, I often turn my attention to writing about topics of interest to students in a way that is accessible to them. One of the regular tasks of university chaplains is delivering invocations and benedictions at official functions. I usually dread these occasions because of their formality and the performance anxiety that goes along with them. I also find naming and praying to "God" in a way that includes everyone and offends no one to be difficult. For large and formal functions, such as commencements and the meetings of the board of trustees, I have given up trying to find the all-inclusive name. Instead, I call upon what I think are sacred and holy qualities without giving them a proper name.

In the invocation for a recent commencement ceremony, I tried to express thankfulness for "grace"—the different ways in which each of us is favored—and to remind us of our responsibility to build communities in which these differences are welcomed and developed. "Grace in community" is central to the Old and New Testaments, as evident in the often quoted "Peaceable Kingdom" passage from the Book of Isaiah (11:6) where "the wolf shall dwell with the lamb"[1] and in Paul's Letter to the Romans (12:4-6) that says, "For as in one body we have many members" and are "individually members of one another, having gifts that differ according to the grace given to us, let us use them."[2] But I chose to avoid the terms of any particular faith in favor of language that could be heard and understood by those of any or no specific faith:

Difference and similarity
enrich us,
and connect us to this place
and to these people.

Difference and similarity
are the basis for
unity as well as separateness.

With them we can be our own person—
but absolutely connected.

We all don't need to do the same thing,
but we do need a community in which to do it.

For the benediction, I chose to work with the image of God's spirit as breath or wind that creates and transforms. The creation story in the Book of Genesis says that "in the beginning, . . . the spirit [or wind] of God was moving over the face of the waters" (1:1-2) and that "God formed the human of dust from the ground and breathed into its nostrils the breath of life; and the human became a living being" (2:7).[3] The Jewish philosopher Martin Buber premises his classic treatise, *I and Thou,* on the image of God's spirit as breath:

> Spirit is not in the I, but between I and Thou. It is not like the blood that circulates in you, but like the air in which you breathe. Man lives in the spirit, if he is able to respond to his Thou. He is able to, if he enters into relation with his whole being. Only in virtue of his power to enter into relation is he able to live in the spirit.[4]

The Buddhist monk Thich Nhat Hanh reinforces the universal holiness of breath: "Our breathing is the link between our body and mind. . . . By concentrating on our breathing, 'In' and 'Out,' we bring body and mind back together, and become whole again."[5] As with the invocation, I avoided terms associated with any one faith and aimed to capture images of breath-change-relationship-life:

Life is a breath
taken in, held, and let out.

Catch your breath,
find your voice.

Breathe into others,
and take their breath.

With them make a song
and let the wind catch your feet and send you flying.

The last line paraphrases a verse from "Wild Night" by Van Morrison, a songwriter whom I and many students like.[6]

   Less frequently, I attempt to include the many names for God instead of using neutral language. Recently a Jewish student asked me to help him organize an Interfaith Gathering for Peace. He told me, "I want to create a prayer service in a neutral space where people of all faiths, traditional and nontraditional, can gather to plug into the common spirit of peace for this world." He invited Muslim, Jewish, Christian, Buddhist, Pagan, Unitarian, and Quaker students. I wrote and read the following prayer at the service:

Adonai of Israel
Allah of Islam
Atma of Brahma
Bodhi of Buddha
God in Christ
Goddess of Life

Breathe into us your breath.
Breathe into us your life.

Create us again in your image,
female and male,
various and diverse.

Encourage us to embrace difference
as a force that enriches
rather than threatens
our efforts to create a peaceful and just world.

Put before us
the choice between life and death
and help us to choose Life, Shalom,
Sakina, Moksha, Nirvana, Harmony, Peace on Earth.

Afterward, in a note thanking me for helping him with the event, he said the prayer "honored all the traditions and their names for the Source of Life in the Spirit of Peace" and "was authentic and from the heart."

But students are not always satisfied—and rightfully so—with neutral or inclusive language about God that does not get at and discuss the different representations of God and reasons for them. Even though my main interest is in getting students to develop their own understanding of God, they sometimes grow impatient with my approach and want to know precisely how and why I image God. I welcome their pressure, and the following piece is an effort to respond to their questions.[7]

BUT WHO DO YOU SAY THAT I AM?

The Bible tells me who God is not with clear definitions, but within the tension of questioning and answering. The Bible does not give me a tidy package of "God" that I can carry around with me and rely on to solve my assorted problems. Instead, the Bible gives me the responsibility to engage God and to know God through dialogue, discussion, argument, and process. God is not a problem-solver for me, but a problem-poser and often a problem. And the Bible places much of the responsibility for solving those problems on me.

My interpretation of the biblical God may seem "radical" in the sense of being drastic, extreme, or off-beat. But it is not. It does not come from digging into remote passages, looking for hidden meaning, reading between the lines, or twisting words and phrases. Instead, it is found in the Bible's central stories; and I read the passages from those stories at face-value and not out of context. If my interpretation is "radical," it is so in the other meaning of the word which has to do with what is fundamental, essential, basic—the "root" of the Bible.[8]

An Old Testament Answer

My primary source for knowing who God is is the Exodus story, particularly Moses' encounter with God.[9] After telling Moses that "I have seen the affliction of my people who are in Egypt and have come down to deliver them out of the hand of the Egyptians," God says, "I will send you to Pharaoh that you may bring forth my people, the children of Israel, out of Egypt." Moses then goes through a litany of doubts, insecurity, apprehension, objection, and avoidance. Why me? Who am I to do this? They won't believe me. They won't listen to me. I am not a good speaker. But God reassures, explains, and provides.

Among the excuses that Moses offers is his ignorance about God's identity. Who is this God who is asking him to take on the responsibility of leading slaves out of bondage? Moses says to God, "If I come to the Israelites and say to them, 'God has sent me to you,' and they ask me what your name is, what shall I say to them?" And God says to Moses, "I AM WHO I AM. Tell them, 'I AM has sent me to you.'" And then God also says, "Tell them, 'YHWH, the God of your ancestors, has sent me to you.' This is my name for ever."

The Hebrew words for "I AM WHO I AM" can also be translated as "I am what I am" or "I will be what I will be." Their use here as a name for God depends on and stems from the Israelite name for God, YHWH, which is derived from the Hebrew verb for "to be."[10]

The Exodus story is central to the Old Testament. The stories that come before it lead up to and anticipate it; and the stories that come after it refer to and build on it. God's choice of Moses and Moses' response to God provide us with fundamental information about God and our relationship with God. In this foundational biblical story we are told by our God that God is not a static, unchanging entity, but an active verb of being in past, present, and future tense. And our relationship with our God is not one of unquestioning obedience, but of honest uncertainty, insecurity, questioning, protest, and negotiation.

The Old Testament puts forth a relationship between humans and the divine that is dialogical, not monological. God does not speak to silent, unresponsive people. Instead, people are expected to answer, doubt, challenge, and interrogate God. In other places throughout the Old Testament, these question-and-answer dialogues with God are rarely tame, laid back, casual conversations. And the New Testament continues this tradition of encounters with the divine that are challenging, emotional, and tension-filled.

A New Testament Answer

One New Testament story in particular is helpful for gaining a better understanding of our relationship with the God of the Bible. The story is told three times—once in each of the Gospels of Matthew, Mark, and Luke.[11] It takes place during the heightened activity of Jesus' ministry as he is traveling with his disciples and speaking to various groups of people. On their way to a village, Jesus asks his disciples, "Who do the people say that I am?" They tell him, "Some say you are John the Baptist; others say Elijah; and still others say you are one of the prophets who has risen." Then the push comes as Jesus asks, "But who do you say I am?" The story turns on these two small, yet powerful words, "but" and "you," as it shifts from questions about popular perception to personal knowledge. Not all of the disciples are ready to respond. Instead of the collective response to his first question, only one disciple, Peter, answers with, "You are the Christ of God." The second question is a lot more difficult and more strongly put. The sharp turn to personal responsibility for knowing about God and the apparent difficulty of gaining such knowledge give the story its importance.

But this importance is given another dimension with a final sentence: "And he charged them to tell no one about him." The knowledge and name of God that we gain in dialogue with God is indeed personal, private, protected, and not to be shared indiscriminately. In the Old Testament story, also, the name for God is camouflaged as a proper noun that reads as verb. The confusion and ambivalence are intentional and protective, and traditionally Jews have regarded the proper name YHWH as too special to pronounce. The Hebrew word "Adonai," meaning "the Lord," is usually substituted.

We protect our relationships with God because their meaning is peculiar and particular to us instead of universal, general, and common. As a person or people we keep the name and knowledge of our God within or among us because it is unique and special to us. The biblical God is not a God for all at once but for each at their times of need. God seems to interact neither with the mass of humanity as one nor with only one chosen person or people. God interacts instead with many chosen individuals and groups of people. We are chosen to interact with and know God not to the exclusion of the others nor in the same way as others. We are chosen in different ways, at different times, and in different company. We preserve, protect, and cherish the meaning of how, why, and when we are chosen; and we do not impose that meaning on others.

A Current Answer

These two stories from the Old and New Testaments tell us that the biblical God is an active verbal ever-presence who engages us and dialogues with us at those times when something is bothering God and/or bothering us. The name of our God and our negotiations and relationship with our God have a special meaning for us that renders us silent about God's name, but confident of God's everlasting presence and interaction with us. To express these qualities, I borrow and combine one sentence from the Exodus story with one sentence from the Jesus story and follow them with three lines from a "Kore Chant" written for the Spring and Fall Equinox by the Goddess theologian Starhawk.[12] I intentionally move from biblical to non-biblical passages because I think the chant effectively captures the unspoken, eternal, constant qualities of the biblical God:

> I Am Who I Am.
> But who do you say I am?
> Her name cannot be spoken,
> Her face was not forgotten,
> Her power is to open,
> Her promise can never be broken.

The image of Goddess need not be seen as opposed to that of God, but as complementary and enriching. The importance of change associated with the Old Testament and New Testament God is active in Starhawk's chant as well:

> She changes everything She touches,
> and Everything She touches, changes.

And she also emphasizes our responsibility to be open to and to make change:

Change is, touch is; Touch is, change is.
Change us! Touch us! Touch us! Change us!

If the Goddess image is a strange one for you, or if it has negative associations for you, Starhawk's definition may make the image more accessible and useful. When she speaks in public and people ask for an image of the Goddess, she tells them to "turn and look at the person sitting next to them."[13]

OPEN LETTERS

Occasionally, I also write a letter to the student newspaper. A few years ago, for example, I wanted to address the stigma of identifying as Christian that some students feel on our campus. There is a broad acceptance of personal spirituality and Eastern religions, but a benign, yet restrictive, stereotyping and rejection of Christianity that typically goes unchallenged here. I used my own experience as a point of departure for discussing the issue more broadly:

An Open Letter to Students:

A lot of my friends think I'm crazy to be a Christian. And many of my queer friends think it's downright stupid. A joke among queer Christians is that it's often easier to come out as gay than to come out as Christian.

Christianity certainly has a bad record when it comes to persecution, oppression, and rigid dogma. Armies have gone forth to kill thousands in the name of Jesus Christ. And Christian moralists have a way of excluding and condemning anyone who doesn't believe as they do.

But the same can be said of any of the other organized religions—Judaism, Islam, Buddhism, and Hinduism. Each has a bloody, imperialist, exclusivist past and present.

It's wise to be suspicious of any religious tradition, because our suspicion may lead us to examine it carefully, take it more seriously, and understand it more fully. The problem is when we dismiss a religion without exploring it thoughtfully.

Because we live in a culture that is predominantly Christian, Christianity may seem to us a bit too overbearing. So, we may find ourselves looking more favorably on the other less familiar religions that don't have such direct influence and control of our lives. But a study of the others will surface sooner or later the same problems that Christianity poses.

Of course, each of the religions offers a set of basic principles on which a life of goodness, fairness, peace, and inclusion can be built. But the ease with which these principles are discarded is indeed bothersome.

Right now, for example, the Christian Right in this country is effectively campaigning to legalize antigay discrimination. Because of its loss of influence in the abortion debate and since the "fall of communism," it has turned its massive fund-raising, propaganda, and organizational ability against queer people. One wonders why "good" Christians are so intent on marginalizing and victimizing people.

At times like these, it's tempting to dismiss all Christians as homophobes and bigots; so, I think it's very important for those Christians who aren't intolerant to identify themselves and declare what kind of Christians they are.

Popular opinion may see Christianity as the exclusive province of evangelical, fundamentalist, or conservative Christians. Somehow, it's easier to lump all Christians into that blend of categories than to deal with the complexity and apparent contradictions of various Christian identities, such as moderate, liberal, progressive, revolutionary, and radical Christians and post-Christians.

I think that these latter kinds of Christians are often too timid and too reluctant to come out, identify, and practice. Because many sense that the campus environment doesn't reward and even stigmatizes Christian identity, it takes a bit of confidence, courage, and risk to put oneself out there as a known Christian. An expression of recognition and support among Christians and some increased awareness and acceptance within the general community would help.

I think the personal and social stakes are too high not to challenge misconceptions and not to assert what's most important to oneself. Progressive Christians have some work to do—both for themselves and for the general community of which they're a part.

To do this kind of work, I usually turn to the Bible for some guidance. The central story and theme in the Old Testament is about freedom from oppression. After the Hebrews are freed from slavery in Egypt, God tells them to love and welcome the stranger among them because they themselves were once strangers in Egypt. Later, the prophets Amos and Micah criticize the development of extravagant rituals and ceremonies and remind the people instead "to do justice, to love kindness, and to walk humbly with your God."

In the New Testament, Jesus begins his ministry by standing up in synagogue and reading a passage by the prophet Isaiah: "The Spirit of God is upon me to set at liberty those who are oppressed." Later, a lawyer presses him to say what the greatest commandment is. He says the first is to love your God with all your might, and the second is like it, "You shall love your neighbor as yourself."

To me these seem to be excellent guidelines and models for living as a Christian within any community. I think we should insist that these are the principles that we as Christians should practice and that it is this kind of practice that identifies us as Christian. We need to be clearer about why we're Christian and what being a Christian means to us. We should feel proud to put forth these Christian principles and to make sure that we practice them.

The response from students was positive. Gay, lesbian, and bisexual students said they felt a measure of relief about not having to separate and hide their other identities; but the predominant response was from nongay students. Many felt encouraged to deal with their own particular peer situations as I had with mine. Because I was candid about my own personal experience and identity, students felt free to talk with me about their own experiences and identity issues, however different they may be from my own.

Here and at my previous college, I have worked directly with gay students in a counseling capacity and to sponsor programs. At the Catholic college I helped students form a gay caucus and support group; and in my current position I have sponsored lectures, panel discussions, and social events. However, over the years I find myself working less directly with gay students and gay issues. Students experiencing the initial difficulties with coming out continue to ask me for help, but students active in the gay community are content to know that I am here as an openly gay chaplain and professor and do not tend to seek me out for help and guidance. Nongay students do so with increasing frequency.

Although anchored in my own identity and experience as a gay man, my ministry is oriented more broadly and my most engaging connections and serious interactions are with nongay students. A few years ago some nongay men approached me about organizing a group to discuss issues of masculinity. These men did not seek me out because they saw our experience as similar, but because they know I will take their experience seriously and encourage them to discuss it. I am amused and pleased that, although I had expected be a role model for gay students, I have become much more so for nongay students. This development has let me better understand what makes a good role model for students—and it is not necessarily someone who matches their experience and identity. The role model on-the-shelf that I am for most gay students is one that I find less engaging, challenging, and helpful than the interactive role model who is developing a process for self-discovery with others whose experiences are different than my own.

I think students are often attracted to adults who are different from themselves, who bring out their individuality rather than provide a model for it. The differences we have with students may be our best resource for relating to and helping them. I suspect that many faculty and staff who are nongay may be better resources for gay students than I am, because they may be more sensitive to many of their personal issues that I have already processed a number of times and may tend to catalogue without a sharp enough ear to special needs and nuances. Our differences with students may be a resource that allows us to listen to them more carefully. I have found that students are looking less for a mirror image of themselves or for experts on their special needs and more for someone with these qualities: personal transparency, willingness to listen, reluctance to judge, and interest in helping others to develop the skills to discover and meet their needs.

Because I have talked with students about their feelings, ideas, and experiences for a number of years, I also attempt to write about some academic topics from their viewpoint. I realize the danger in assuming that one can authentically speak about or from within the experience of another, but I feel that many topics are not accessible to students because they are presented too abstractly. I also think that professors usually write in the style they adopted for their doctoral dissertations. This style is fine for communicating with one's dissertation committee of advanced scholars, but it does not connect directly with undergraduate students. The following is my attempt to talk about the complicated scholarly issue of biblical authorship by using language and experience that is familiar to college students.[14]

GENESIS

Imagine that an important person in your family, your grandmother, has just died. Although you respected and loved this person a great deal, you had never gotten to know her intimately. When you were very young your mother and father moved far away from the family neighborhood, so your time with your grandmother was on infrequent and short visits.

Now with the occasion of her death you feel great loss not only because the person was wonderful and special, but also because there was so much about her that you didn't get the chance to know. For this reason, attending the funeral, even though it's a long plane flight away and will take you away from school for at least a week, is very important to you.

On the plane flight you feel regret even more strongly for not having known your grandmother better. As you recall the usual remarks and stories told about her, they lack the depth, clarity, and reality that you feel a strong need to know now. You decide, therefore, that after the funeral you'll purposely spend time with certain relatives and friends of your grandmother—to listen and probe, to collect the information and insights about your grandmother, to round out and give substance to the limited picture you feel you have of her, to let you capture the person in a way that will be lasting for you.

At the reception after the funeral you seek out and talk to your Aunt Jane, your grandmother's younger sister. Talking with her is easy, because Jane is approachable and relaxed. The two of you find two lawn chairs outside and chat comfortably for a long time.

Jane is a no-nonsense kind of person. She has a way of getting to the point without a lot of flowery details but with a lot of human sensitivity. Her stories about your grandmother are clear, simple, and yet get to the heart of who she was as a real person.

Jane is a social worker, and her skills and experience become apparent as she describes your grandmother's strengths and weaknesses, vulnerability and determination. She's able to talk sympathetically and objectively about the mistakes your grandmother made and the problems she had. The rather one-dimensional image of your grandmother as great and wonderful takes on greater depth for you as Jane tells you about the difficulties she had as an immigrant coming to this country, the quarrels she had with various relatives about going to law school, the time she almost lost her job or almost left your grandfather, the sadness she felt when your mother and father moved away from the neighborhood.

From Jane's stories you learn that your grandmother was a person with concerns quite like your own. You feel that the problems you're having with your boyfriend or girlfriend, with your grades, with your parents, with choosing a career are the kinds of things that your grandmother dealt with also.

Later that day you also have a chance to talk with Elliot, one of the young lawyers who had worked in your grandmother's law firm for many years. The conversation is congenial, but unlike the one with Jane, not as casual and lengthy. Instead of finding a comfortable place to sit and chat, the two of you talk while standing next to the refreshments table.

Elliot is not a good storyteller like Jane. Elliot doesn't create a weave of human details about your grandmother. Elliot quite obviously admired and was in awe of your grandmother. His conversation with you is made up of the spectacular parts of her professional life— the great causes she championed, the legal cases of poor people she won, the unpopular issues she brought into the public arena.

Elliot provides the details about the great civic woman you had always heard your grandmother to be. He gives substance to the popular, traditional perception of your grandmother. He isn't subtle or psychological like Jane and doesn't give you much to reflect on or puzzle about. He doesn't mention the hitches, detours, and doubts she had. His is a glowing account of the great things that she had done. Elliot gives you her public image. When you ask about the time when your parents moved away, Elliot gives the response that people at the office heard, not the one she confided to close friends: he says she simply supported your parents to make their own decisions. Elliot tells you what your grandmother said to the world, while Jane gave you the sadness, loneliness, and personal happiness that your grandmother experienced.

Although your conversation with Jane and Elliot give you two different sides of your grandmother, in your third conversation with Peter, your cousin, you find it difficult to get any kind of a picture of your grandmother.

It isn't because Peter isn't willing to talk—quite the opposite— he's eager to take you aside and give you any number of details about your and his grandmother.

Peter is not much older than yourself. He hasn't had the intimacy and time with your grandmother that Jane had nor Elliot's experience as her colleague and co-worker. Much of his information is second-hand rather than personal.

Peter is also a librarian, with skills and interest in collecting things and putting and keeping them in order.

From Peter, therefore, you get an assortment of well-organized facts about your grandmother. He rambles off the family tree back to great-great-grandparents in Italy and forward to the youngest grand-child. Peter has all her dates—when she came to this country, when she graduated, got married, argued her first case. He can tell you what her publicly stated positions were on a variety of issues and where she was and what she was doing at critical times. Unlike Jane with her personal insights and Elliot with his highlights of your grandmother's achievements, Peter seems to have a nicely organized body of data. About your parents' moving away, he seems to know little more than when it happened, where they went, and that it was simply because one of your parents was transferred by their company. The emotional costs or the significance of that event are not a part of his account. Peter's remarks have neither the subtle narrative quality of Jane's nor the boastful heroism of Elliot's. Peter's conversation after a while tends to be ponderous and boring and you find yourself trying to fig-ure out how you can get back to the refreshment table and other peo-ple.

On your way home on the six-hour plane flight from California to New York you think back on these three conversations with Jane, Elliot, and Peter and realize that they are important sources for filling in to some degree what you felt lacking on your flight out. The regret or sadness you were feeling on your way to the funeral has been alleviated somewhat.

As you think about the conversations, certain parts of them are par-ticularly striking and surface more intensely than other parts. Various parts of the conversations mean more to you than others and domi-nate your thoughts. You take out your notebook and begin to jot down and record what seem to you to be significant remarks, stories, obser-vations, and facts. You begin to organize them into an order that makes sense to you, that tells your grandmother's story in a way that is meaningful for you, that begins to capture who you understand your grandmother to have been. You arrange Jane, Elliot, and Peter's remarks into a single story about your grandmother that remembers her in the best way for you and that may tell others about her as well. Perhaps Peter's remarks will serve as the nuts and bolts of the story. They may provide the information for introductory paragraphs that serve to give the date, place, and specific details for grasping the personal anecdotes that come from Jane's remarks. Peter's remarks may lend themselves to giving your story structure and organization. His remarks may provide the dates and order of events—the skeleton. Elliot and Jane's remarks may be used alternately or as complements. The public image and the personal feelings of your grandmother, the lawyer and the person, may be combined to create the tension or dynamic that captures the wholeness of your grandmother as you've come to understand her.

Even though the three sources you use are not your own, you have the power to edit and arrange them in such a way as to create another store entirely. What you choose to use from the conversations, what you choose to emphasize, and the order in which you put it will reflect what you consider to be important about your grandmother. Your finished product may be shaped by what you want others to know about her. What you put together on the plane flight home and finalize in later sessions may be the only information that your children and other relatives will have for knowing who their great grandmother was.

I have created this scenario as a way to try to introduce Genesis, the first book of the Old Testament, and I have tried to imagine a situation in which you are faced with the same task as what biblical scholars have identified as the *redactor* of the Book of Genesis.

A redactor is one who revises, edits, draws up, frames, or puts into suitable literary form an unorganized collection of stories and information. On the way home on the plane you were redacting. You were selecting parts of the conversations you had heard, and you were arranging them into a coherent or whole story.

Someone reading your story—no matter how skillfully you had put the parts together—may still be able to notice that there seems to be a variety of voices within your story. The boastfulness of Elliot and the psychological insights of Jane may give a richness to the story, but they may also seem juxtaposed or distinct; and when you draw on Peter's catalog of facts and dates, the various sources for your story may become even more apparent. Maybe you decide to preserve the informal language of Aunt Jane when you record her stories because it seems so appropriate for the kind of stories she's telling, whereas such informality would not be appropriate to the more formal tributes that Elliot made to your grandmother. Perhaps you decide to allow for this apparent inconsistency of language within your story because it allows for the story to reflect more accurately who your grandmother really was.

Almost two hundred years ago, scholars began to recognize this kind of variety as they studied the Book of Genesis. That it had not been noticed before or remarked on may indicate how skillfully and effectively various sources can be woven together into one story by a redactor.

In noting what nineteenth-century biblical scholars began to notice as they read Genesis, I want to make some comparisons with your experience as a redactor and the story that you might have produced about your grandmother.

First of all, scholars noticed that the characters in the Book of Genesis—Eve and Adam, Cain and Abel, Noah, Sarah and Abraham, Isaac, Rachel and Jacob, for instance—are not always depicted in the same way.

Some of the stories about them are clear, simple, and direct, capturing in their simplicity the whole of life, its heights and depths. These stories are attributed to a source that scholars have come to call the Yahwist or J. In your story about your grandmother it would be like the source we have called your Aunt Jane. Like Jane, the Yahwist or J is both a good storyteller and a good psychologist. The Yahwist presents the riddles and conflicts, mistakes and muddles of *human* acts, the secrets of the human heart, the things that make life difficult, challenging and interesting. It is from the Yahwist source that the redactors seem to have taken those vibrant stories about sin and suffering, marital relations, sibling rivalry, and international disputes that make Genesis memorable. By the Yahwist, God, too, is portrayed more humanly than by the other sources. In the Yahwist accounts God actually walks in the garden, physically closes the doors of the ark for Noah, and descends to inspect the Tower of Babel.

Just as your story about your grandmother relies on Jane for most of its material and for its liveliness, so the redactor of Genesis draws most heavily from the Yahwist source and its stories linger as the most memorable in Genesis.

The second source for the Book of Genesis is the Elohist or E source. It's comparable to Elliot in your story about your grandmother.

The Elohist's stories are not told as well as the Yahwist's. They are less finely woven with interesting *human* details. They tend to emphasize *divine* deeds—the spectacular and miraculous—and don't engage us or cause us to ponder them personally.

Unlike the Yahwist, the Elohist does not depict God as in the midst of humans. In the Elohist's stories God's appearances and movements on earth are limited. God calls down from heaven and sends angels down, but is for the most part removed from earth.

The Elohist depicts God as Elliot depicted your grandmother—as a powerful, popular, spectacular figure who seemed to work miracles, but not as a down-to-earth *human* being.

To understand the differences between the Yahwist and Elohist sources in Genesis, we can briefly compare the various parts of the story of Joseph with the Coat of Many Colors.

You may remember that Joseph was betrayed by his brothers who sold him into slavery and let him be taken away to Egypt. His brothers then told their father that he had been killed and devoured by a wild beast. This part of the Joseph story is told by the Yahwist. It is full of human issues—rivalry, lying, betrayal, family relationships.

The continuing story about Joseph in Genesis shifts to his life in Egypt where he rises from slavery to a position of power and influence. This is the Elohist's story; and instead of revolving around human intrigue, Joseph's rise is achieved through advice that he receives from God in his dreams. For the Elohist, as for Elliot in your story, the spectacular and miraculous are featured over human action and feelings, and like the redactor of Genesis you rely less on the Elliot-type resource and more on the Aunt Jane-type. You find the human grandmother more compelling than the public figure.

The third source of the Book of Genesis is what scholars have come to call the Priestly or P source. This, of course, is the equivalent of Peter in the story about your grandmother. Like Peter, the P source is the youngest or most recent, dating from around 500 to 400 B.C.; like your Aunt Jane, the Yahwist is the oldest, dating from around 950 to 900 B.C. Scholars call this source the Priestly source because the information provided by it seems to come from priests who were scribes, recorders, and keepers of records. Peter, as you may remember from your grandmother's funeral, is a librarian. The concern of Priestly or P material in Genesis is form and order, and as with your story about your grandmother it lends form and order to the Book of Genesis. The language, like Peter's to you, tends to be succinct, ponderous, pedantic, and lacking in artistry. The Priestly material is devoid of vivid narration. Here there is little interest in depicting humans in actual circumstances. The P accounts are colorless. They focus not on human experience and human history, but provide lists and specifications.

For example, in Genesis genealogical lists of descendants and generations are put at the beginnings of the stories drawn from the Yahwist source. The lists are the work of the P source and are used by the redactor to introduce, frame, and put in order the various stories. The story of Noah, for example, is preceded by his birth in the line of biblical ancestors. In this way the redactor connects him with other characters who are the subjects of other stories in the Book of Genesis. It establishes Noah's place in the lineage of biblical characters, but it contributes little to the substance of the story that follows. It gives the reader some bearings and provides order more than content. For the same reasons, such details of date, time, and place are borrowed from P to connect and give identity to what would otherwise seem to be unrelated stories.

As you may have used Peter in your story about your grandmother, so the redactor of Genesis used P to organize, form transitions, and lend continuity to the collected stories by the Yahwist and Elohist.

The contrast between the Yahwist and the Priestly sources is shown most clearly in the creation stories. As you begin to read the Book of Genesis you will notice that there seem to be two creation stories.

The first seems to be from the Priestly source. It talks about the *order* in which the world was created:

1. light/darkness
2. heaven
3. waters
4. dry land
5. vegetation
6. stars, moon, sun
7. living creatures
   - birds
   - sea monsters
   - cattle, farm beasts
   - humans (male and female together at the same time)

This order of creation was spread out over six days.

P's interest in the order of creation is obvious here. Any kind of a human interest story is absent. Humans are simply mentioned as created in God's image and given dominion over the plants and animals which had been created before the humans.

The Book of Genesis, however, then takes an abrupt and sharp shift to tell a different kind of story. The break and difference with the P story is most apparent because man (this time without woman) is being created again—and this time not simply in the image of God. God here is breathing God's own breath into earth and forming man from it as a potter would shape clay. This personally involved God is the God of the Yahwist.

This story is also different from the previous one because man is formed before woman, and instead of being given dominion over plants and animals which have already been created, animals are created one after the other as company for the lonely man. Woman is that which finally is created as suitable company.

Not only is it apparent that we have two different stories here, since the order of creating human and animals is different, but the central interest of each story is different as well.

The Priestly story is concerned with the ordering and numbering of creation; the Yahwist story is concerned with the human situation—the loneliness of man, and as we know from the Eve and Adam story, getting in trouble, marital relationships, childrearing, and sibling rivalry. This is the kind of story typical of the Yahwist, and it is the kind of story that you got from Aunt Jane.

You may be asking—and I hope you are—"Wouldn't it be possible for you or the redactor of Genesis to have put the three sources together in such a way as to make the three sources undetectable and the whole story smoothly coherent?" The answer is that Genesis is indeed remarkably well-redacted and coherent. That its three sources were not noted until the nineteenth century may well be proof of that.

But we must also allow for a redactor's choice to intend variety and nuance within a whole. Perhaps the choice to preserve various voices and styles was intentional. Consider the three stories you heard about your grandmother's response to your parents' moving away. It would be hard to combine the three stories into one, because the understanding and language expressed in each are so different. Each story has its own merit, its own valid point, its own unity. After playing with them for a while you may decide to let the three stand, to let them follow one another and provide various viewpoints. You and the redactor of Genesis may have made decisions not to flatten all the sources, but to preserve the texture, variability, and richness of viewpoints and expressions.

In studying the stories in Genesis, we can appreciate the uniqueness of the stories and the part they play in the whole book. We will need to keep in mind also that our efforts to examine and take apart this document may violate certain intentions and purposes of the original redactors. Our efforts need to be guided with both a willingness to inquire and explore as well as to relax and appreciate the stories.

I realize there are problems and dangers in trying to speak to, from within, and out of other people's experience. Careful study of and sensitive listening to others may not be enough to overcome my own biases and conceits as I try to empathize with their experience. But, as human beings, I do not think we can afford not to try to "see faithfully from another's point of view."[15] Community, relationship, and interaction seem to me to depend on our ability and willingness to empathize and to try to put ourselves into other frames of reference. We also need to think of our efforts not as final products that fail or succeed, but as steps in an ongoing process in which others respond to our efforts with constructive criticism, with appreciation, and with their own efforts to interpret our experiences and to put themselves into our frames of reference.

Chapter 6

Creating Worship

LOOSENING UP AND MEETING NEEDS

When I began my current position as a university chaplain, I inherited a 10:00 Sunday morning worship service with an attendance of ten to twelve students. I knew that my efforts to increase attendance would go against an almost universal given of college life—sleeping in on Sunday. By my second semester I had shifted the service to 4:30 in the afternoon, and attendance doubled. From conversations with students, though, I could tell that this time was not ideal either. Sundays for many college students follow a similar pattern—catching up on lost sleep from late-night studying and partying, feeling guilty for not having attended to weekend studying, and preparing for the upcoming week's classes. Going to church tends to add to rather than alleviate the anxiety of catching up. I wanted to find a better time that would allow and encourage students to focus on their spiritual lives.

I also came to my new job from a "social justice" religious tradition. I was accustomed to worship services that address social problems and our responsibility to solve them. Because this university is known for its attention to social problems, I assumed that my work as a chaplain would follow suit. I came to discover, however, that students want and need more attention to their personal, emotional lives. Because students are actively involved in community and political work, they do not need to be told to be more responsible. In fact, I often counsel students to ease up on some of their commitments to social problems because they take on too much responsibility. They are also serious and enthusiastic about their studies and challenge their professors and each other intellectually. In such a cerebral and socially responsible environment, affective needs are often not taken seriously enough, even though personal and familial relationships, fear of failure, loneliness, stress, and pressure are major concerns for students. These are the concerns I began to address more and more.

When I began my position I also continued the form and style of traditional Protestant services: invocation, an Old Testament and a New Testament reading, sermon, pastoral prayer, benediction, three hymns dispersed throughout the service, and organ music. For each service I prepared and rehearsed my sermon and the liturgy days in advance. I wore a suit and tie. If I made a "mistake" or if something went wrong, such as a hymn that did not work, I was upset with myself; but I noticed that students seemed to appreciate mistakes and incidental informalities. They were more willing to experiment and did not demand precision and perfection. They wanted to relax in a casual context. After I stopped wearing my suit and tie, became more conversational and less rehearsed, and welcomed more informality into the services, students came in larger numbers and put more of themselves into the services. Rather than the conventional role of the minister as an authority in the center or at the head of the people, I found and took my place in their midst—not completely as one of them, because to do so would be patronizing and dishonest, but as one who listened before he spoke and spoke from his heart rather than from prepared notes.

The overriding interest of most Protestant students at my university can be characterized as seeking spiritual development that is not contingent on a single form of organized religion. Their interest is not unlike that of non-Protestant students who are interested in their spirituality but are agnostic, atheistic, or nonaffiliated. When Protestant students do want to discuss their own tradition or denomination, the preferred format is a roundtable discussion with others from other denominations and faiths, not simply with different kinds of Protestants, but with Jews, Catholics, Muslims, Hindus, and Buddhists. My primary effort has been to find a time and to design a service that would bring together different people to explore different religious expressions—to create a pattern of worship for relating across our differences to find what we have in common.

STUMBLING ONTO A SOLUTION

In the fall semester of my third year, I organized a memorial service for the African-American poet and essayist Audre Lorde. Lorde was not affiliated with the university, but her work was important to many students and her death caused much sadness. I wanted to find a time for the service that would not conflict with an already crammed weekly schedule. I chose the 5:30 to 6:30 p.m. slot on a Wednesday and provided a buffet so that people would not have to worry about missing supper. I planned a simple service. I asked several students to select and bring pieces of Lorde's work to read. A visiting faculty member whose research involved African-American women writers agreed to say a few words about how much Lorde's work meant to her personally. I arranged for one of the women's a capella groups on campus to perform songs by the African-American women's group Sweet Honey in the Rock. There was a time for silent reflection. I made brief introductory and closing comments and asked people to take a flower from the large arrangement with them when they left. The service was informal and relaxed. People were touched by the calm, meditative, intimate mood and stayed for a long time afterward to eat and hang out.

One student said to me, "It's too bad we don't have something like this every week." Then it dawned on me. This was the kind of weekly service that I had been struggling to create. Many other pieces of what students had been telling me during the previous two years fell together. They needed a set-aside, special time in the middle of the week—not on the weekend. To be able to step away from everyday busyness and to step into a quiet time and place to relax was what students had been telling me they wanted, but I had not quite heard or understood the actual form that meeting their needs would take. I shifted the weekly service from Sunday afternoon to Wednesday evening.

For the first semester, fewer students attended the Wednesday night services than had attended the Sunday services. Even the best planned and most necessary changes come slowly! As news about the service spread by word of mouth, attendance did increase—not slowly by ones and twos, but by big jumps of ten to fifteen. By the middle of the next semester it was up to about forty, then to sixty-five, until it leveled off after three years to about 100 students. The following is a description of the service.

VESPERS

It bears the name Vespers, which means evening service. In publicity and announcements the service is described as "an informal time to relax, discuss spirituality, create ritual, and enjoy dinner in a comfortable setting." Two aspects of the memorial service for Lorde have remained constant at every Vespers: we have a flower arrangement from which people are asked to take one or two flowers with them when they leave for themselves or for someone who was not at the service; and we close with a delicious, nutritious, free meal. The service is scheduled for 5:30 p.m. but always starts ten minutes late. Our chapel has a stage at the front on which we all sit. Students straggle in by ones, twos, and small groups. They leave their coats, shoes, and backpacks in the pews and make their way up onto the stage. Some continue to arrive throughout the service. I encourage them to come when they can and not to worry if they have to be late—and not to feel guilty if they make it only for the meal.

We sit on cushions on the floor in concentric circles around the flower arrangement and a few lighted candles. Cushioned built-in benches form the outer perimeter and accommodate those who cannot or do not want to sit on the floor. With 100 attending, the fit is tight and people are close. The house lights are dim—as students say, "The darker the better." The walls around the stage are windowless, and the feeling on the stage is one of quiet and removal from the rest of the campus. People sit quietly or talk casually with their friends. I ask for announcements of events that are happening on campus. People give the times and dates of parties, concerts, plays, and meetings with which they are involved. By this time there is a settled-in sense that most people have arrived. The "ritual" begins. I often lead it, but more often students lead it with me or by themselves. Once in a while an outside guest leads it.

Each week the ritual is different. It lasts anywhere from fifteen to thirty minutes, occasionally as long as forty-five minutes. As a clergyman, I am familiar with the design and use of ritual in organized religion. I am also familiar with students' disinterest in, rejection of, and rebellion against the rituals of organized religion because of what they see as the repetition, coercion, and hollowness of traditional ritual. I even support and encourage their criticism. But I also know that meaningful rituals can be created.

In his study *The Magic of Ritual,* Tom Driver distinguishes between what he calls "shamanistic" and "priestly" rituals. Priestly rituals are well-organized and routinely performed by officials to maintain order, encourage obedience, and preserve tradition within an institution. The priest is an insider with an interest in maintaining the social order and his position within it. In shamanistic rituals, on the other hand, transformation takes precedent over order. They are not meant to be proper. Variation and enthusiasm, rather than fixed symbolism and liturgical precision, are valued. These rituals tend to be unpredictable, experimental, and uncertain. A shaman is perceived as unconventional or abnormal—an outsider who challenges or ignores the established order. Shamanistic rituals are not without order, but unlike priestly rituals that preserve the old order, shamanistic rituals seek to create new order.[1]

I do not have romantic notions of myself as an inspirational shaman. But as an openly gay clergyperson at a time when most religious bodies are making a lot of noise about not ordaining lesbians and gay men, I am perceived by students as someone who is outside of and challenging the social and religious order. My status reinforces their own questioning, examining, and challenging of organized religion. Also, because I shape my programs to meet their needs rather than to conform to convention, they see me as an ally in their spiritual exploration and search for meaning.

Ritual can be defined as a planned or improvised performance that provides a transistion from daily life into a different context in which everyday concerns and problems are transformed.[2] At Vespers students step out of, reflect on, and create an alternative to their everyday life so that they can return to, change, appreciate, and live it more fully. A key term in this definition is "performance," or what I prefer to call "activity." A ritual must be more than telling people what to do and having people follow along. Each person must feel comfortable and empowered to do, create, or contribute something on their own. Participants should be able to express something personal, not to feel embarrassed or judged, to feel "normal" about what they express. I do not mean "normalcy" that is the product of conforming to the group's expectations, but of having one's particularity or "oddity" welcomed, accepted, and affirmed by the group.

Here is a ritual that worked well: Students are asked to take a chunk of clay from a basket at the edge of the stage before they sit down. There are many different colors to choose from. After announcements, I explain that the ritual will be a series of readings interspersed with pauses and the ringing of a Buddhist gong. I have met with the two students beforehand to select the readings and to discuss our roles in the ritual. The readings will present different images of God. I encourage people to listen to and take each of them seriously, to consider their applicability and relevance to their own feelings, questions, and ideas about the meaning of life. I refer to the theologian Paul Tillich, who said that God is what is ultimately meaningful in one's life and that faith is the state of being ultimately concerned. That which is most important to us is our God, and our lives are most godlike when we embrace, take seriously, and share with others what is most important to us.[3] I ask that they shape and play with their chunks of clay as they listen to the readings and reflect on what is most important to them. The house lights are turned off. The only illumination is provided by two candles held by the readers. The darkness allows students to shape their clay in privacy. I begin the first reading, "Bells of Mindfulness" by the Vietnamese Buddhist monk Thich Nhat Hanh:

In my tradition, we use the temple bells to remind us to come back to the present moment. Every time we hear the bell, we stop talking, stop our thinking, and return to ourselves, breathing in and out, and smiling. Whatever we are doing, we pause for a moment and just enjoy our breathing. Sometimes we also recite this verse:

Listen, listen.
This wonderful sound brings me back to my true self.

When we breathe in, we say, "Listen, listen," and when we breathe out, we say, "This wonderful sound brings me back to my true self."[4]

Pause. Gong. Pause.

Student's Reading
(taken from the Book of Genesis in the Bible)

> God formed the human from the clay of the earth and breathed into its nostrils the breath of life; and the human became a living being.[5]

My Reading
(from the Book of Genesis)

> And God created the human in God's own image; in the image of God, God created the human; male and female God created them.[6]

Pause. Gong. Pause.

Student's Reading
(from the novel Ceremony *by the Native American writer Leslie Marmon Silko)*

> . . .Thought-Woman
> is sitting in her room
> and whatever she thinks about
> appears.
>
> She thought of her sisters,
> . . .
> and together they created the Universe
> this world
> and the four worlds below.
>
> Thought-Woman, the spider,
> named things and
> as she named them
> they appeared.
>
> She is sitting in her room
> thinking of a story now
>
> I'm telling you the story
> she is thinking.[7]

My Reading

>   In the Torah, when God chooses Moses to lead the slaves out of bondage, Moses asks God, "If I come to the people of Israel and say to them, 'The God of your ancestors has sent me to you,' and they ask me, 'What is God's name?,' what shall I say to them?" And God said to Moses, "I AM WHO I AM." God said, "Say this to the people of Israel, I AM has sent me to you."[8]

Pause. Gong. Pause.

Student's Reading

>   Later in Jewish scripture, I AM says, "I have shown you what is good; and what does I AM require of you but to do justice, and to love kindness, and to walk humbly with your God."[9]

My Reading

>   Later still, in Christian scripture, when God is asked how we shall be able to recognize and know God, God responds, "I was hungry and you gave me food; I was thirsty and you gave me drink; I was a stranger and you welcomed me; I was naked and you clothed me; I was sick and you nursed me; I was in prison and you came to me." And the people say, "When did we help you when you were hungry, thirsty, alone, naked, or in prison?" And God said, "When you helped the least of my children, you did it to me."[10]

Pause. Gong. Pause.

Student's Reading
(from "Why I Am a Muslim" by prison chaplain Jimmy Jones)

>   Christianity, as I understood it, did not seem to give enough clear guidance for everyday living. Al-Islam, on the other hand, reflected its consistent emphasis on the ultimate supremacy of God by providing a clear, structured framework for striving to carry out that belief in daily living.

I found, for example, the systematic prayer at required times in the course of each day to be a spiritual anchor in a turbulent, transitory world.

"There is no God except Allah and Muhammad is his Messenger," is the . . . declaration of faith that makes me proud to be a Muslim. I am proud because here we aggressively assert the idea of one God, a single God, to the exclusion of multiple personifications of the divine.

"All praise is due to God." In daily life, I strive to live this ideal. In a society where greed, selfishness, and pride are often looked upon as useful attributes, it is difficult to keep a proper perspective. What sustains me is the knowledge that, in spite of tremendous difficulties in my life, God has blessed me by allowing me to find and come into this beautiful religion.[11]

My Reading
(from Hermann Hesse's novel Siddhartha*)*

When someone is seeking, . . . it happens quite easily that he only sees the thing that he is seeking; that he is unable to find anything, unable to absorb anything, because he is only thinking of the thing he is seeking, because he has a goal, because he is obsessed by his goal. Seeking means: to have a goal; but finding means: to be free, to be receptive, to have no goal. You . . . are perhaps a seeker, for in striving towards your goal, you do not see many things that are under your nose.[12]

Pause. Gong. Pause.

Student's Reading
(from The Sacred Hoop *by Native American author Paula Gunn Allen)*

There is a spirit that pervades everything, that is capable of powerful song and radiant movement, and that moves in and out of the mind. . . . This spirit, this power of intelligence, has many names and many emblems. She appears on the plains, in the forests, in the great canyons, on the mesas, beneath the seas. To her we owe our very breath, and to her our prayers are sent blown on pollen, on corn meal, planted into the earth on feather-sticks, spit onto the water, burned and sent to her on the wind.[13]

My Reading
(paraphrasing from Alice Walker's novel The Color Purple*)*

    Shug tells her friend Celie that we are all born with God inside us, but we still have to search to find God. Shug's first step was to let go of the popular notion of God as the old man in the sky, removed from and above us. She then found God when she felt a part of the trees, the air, birds, and other people. She said that when you feel happy about being a part of, and not separated from everything, you have found God.[14]

Pause. Gong. Pause.

Student's Reading
(from Audre Lorde's collection of essays, Sister Outsider*)*

    For each of us as women, there is a dark place within, where hidden and growing our true spirit rises. . . .

    These places of possibility within ourselves are dark because they are ancient and hidden; they have survived and grown strong through that darkness. Within these deep places, each one of us holds an incredible reserve of creativity and power, of unexamined and unrecorded emotion and feeling. The woman's place of power within each of us . . . is dark, it is ancient, and it is deep.[15] (Reprinted with permission from *Sister Outsider* by Audre Lorde, copyright 1984. Published by the Crossing Press, Santa Cruz, California.)

My Reading
(*from* The Intimate Connection: Male Sexuality, Masculine
Spirituality *by James Nelson*)

To be fully masculine is one of the two ways given to humanity of being fully human. To be fully masculine . . . means embracing the fullness of the revelation that comes through our
male bodies. There is good phallic energy in us which we can
claim and celebrate. It is the earthy phallus: deep, moist, and
sensuous, primitive and powerful. The phallic energy in us is
also solar: penetrating, thrusting, achieving, and with the desire
for self-transcendence. Equally important *and equally male,*
there is good penile energy in us. It is soft, vulnerable, and receptive. It is a peaceful power. It knows that size is not merely
quantitative; more truly, it is that strength of mutuality which
can be enriched by other life without losing its own center.

The orgasmic sexual experience brings its own revelation.
The hard and explosive phallic achievement becomes in an in-
stant the soft, vulnerable tears of the penis. Both are fully male.
Both are deeply grounded in a man's bodily reality. Both dimensions of life are fully present when a man is most human.[16]

Pause. Gong. Pause.

Student's Reading
(*from* Touching Our Strength *by lesbian Christian theologian
Carter Heyward*)

To be really present with another, we must experience ourselves as connected with the other in . . . "mutually empathic
and empowering" ways.

To be mutually empathic and empowering is to learn not only
how to listen and hear, well and deeply, but also how to speak
honestly of ourselves and be heard from the depths of who we
are.[17]

My Reading
(*from* Dreaming the Dark: Magic, Sex and Politics *by the Goddess theologian Starhawk*)

> When I say Goddess I am not talking about a being some-where outside of this world, nor am I proposing a new belief system. I am talking about choosing an attitude: choosing to take this living world, the people and creatures on it, as the ulti-mate meaning and purpose of life, to see the world, the earth, and our lives as sacred.[18]

Pause. Gong. Pause.

Student's Reading
(*from Heyward's* Touching Our Strength)

> Once there was a wise old woman, a witch, who lived in a small village. The children of the village were puzzled by her— her wisdom, her gentleness, her strength, and her magic. One day several of the children decided to fool the old woman. They believed that no one could be as wise as everyone said she was, and they were determined to prove it. So the children found a baby bird and one of them cupped it in his hands and said to his playmates, "We'll ask her whether the bird I have in may hands is dead or alive. If she says it's dead, I'll open my hands and let it fly away. If she says it's alive, I'll crush it in my hands and she'll see that it's dead." And the children went to the old witch and presented her with this puzzle. "Old woman," the child asked, "This bird in my hands—is it dead or alive?" The old woman be-came very still, studied the child's hands, and then looked care-fully into his eyes. "It's in your hands," she said.[19]

The student reader and I then extinguish our candles. In the near total darkness we ask students to pass their shaped clay forward so that people sitting closest to the center can place them around the flower arrangement. The lights are brought up to reveal a wide rang-ing assortment of various images in different colors. I am always de-lighted and impressed by the creativity and originality of students when we do this kind of exercise.

We then pass around the following prayer written by Starhawk. After indicating an imaginary line dividing the group, the student reader and I alternate reading with each side and then together:

Left	Right
Nameless One	of many names
Eternal	and ever-changing One
Who is found nowhere	but appears everywhere
Beyond	and within all.
Timeless	circle of the seasons,
Unknowable mystery	known by all.
Lord of the dance,	Mother of all life,
Be radiant within us,	Engulf us with your love,

Together

See with our eyes, Hear with our ears, Breathe with our nostrils,

Touch with our hands, Kiss with our lips, Open our hearts!

That we may be free at last

Joyful in the single song

Of all that is, was, or shall ever be![20]

We close as usual by passing a candle around and asking each person to give her or his name. Dinner is set up on buffet tables below the stage, students serve themselves, bring their food back up on the stage, and sit in small informal groups. People stay for anywhere from fifteen minutes to an hour depending on meetings, classes, or studies that they must attend to.

Most rituals are not as heavy on readings as this one. Once during the third week of the fall semester, when I knew that frosh were feeling homesick and students generally were missing family and summer friends, the ritual had no readings. As people came in they were asked to pick up a taper and a pinch of clay. After they were settled, I asked that they look around the gathering for those they had never

met or talked to, then to get up, go over, and introduce themselves to a
new person. They then sat down and took turns telling one another
about a person they were missing. After a few minutes, we turned our
attention from the paired conversation back to the whole group. I
asked that they think about the person they were missing and when
ready to go to the center of the circle, to light their taper for this person, and with the pinch of clay to set their taper onto the floor (actually, onto a large sheet of fire-resistant board). Gradually, people got
up to light and set their tapers. The resulting gathering of lighted tapers created a presence of the people we were missing.

The only ritual we repeat is the Planting Ritual. It follows spring
break and honors the various springtime holidays of renewal, change,
liberation. Short introductory readings about Passover, Easter, and
the spring equinox are followed by these two biblical passages:

> Forget the former things; do not dwell on the past. See, I am do-
> ing a new thing! Now it springs up; do you not perceive it?
> (Isaiah 43:18-19)
>
> Arise, my love, my fair one.
>   and come away;
> for lo, the winter is past,
>   the rain is over and gone.
> The flowers appear on the earth,
>   the time of singing has come,
> and the voice of the turtledove
>   is heard in our land.
> The fig tree puts forth its figs,
>   and the vines are in blossom;
>   they give forth fragrance.
> Arise, my love, my fair one,
>   and come away. (Songs of Songs 2: 10-13)[21]

In place of the customary flower arrangement are a pile of potting
soil, flats of small flowering plants, and stacks of small flower pots.
Four large bowls with a candle burning beside each one have been
placed around them. After the readings, I ask people to think of something that they want to let go of, to be done with, to change, to get rid

of. On the way in each had picked up a scrap of paper and a pen, and now they have time to think and write. When I see that people have stopped writing, I ask that they go when ready to one of the bowl-and-candle sets, light their piece of paper, drop it into the bowl, and as it burns think of letting go of whatever they want to let go of. When all have done so and are seated, I (or a student I have asked beforehand) empty the ashes from each bowl onto the pile of potting soil and mix them in. I ask that when ready people select a plant from one the flats and transplant it into one of the pots. I demonstrate how to do it. Small groups of five to seven take turns until everyone has a plant to take back to their room and care for during the rest of the semester. There are plenty of plants left over, so during the meal people can do more potting and bring plants to their friends who were not at the service.

A feature of most rituals is silence or "waiting" time. Many students come to Vespers to get away from such stimulated environments as dorms and dining areas and to spend time by themselves in the company of others who do not require or demand their attention. Waiting to take turns to light their candle or to pot their plant, therefore, cushions an already contemplative service with another opportunity to be alone with one's own thoughts and feelings.

BUT IS VESPERS CHRISTIAN ENOUGH?

From the beginning, Vespers has attracted a mixed crowd of Protestants, Roman Catholics, Jews, Hindus, Buddhists, Muslims, agnostics, and atheists. And I have worked to make the service one that welcomes and encourages this mix. Occasionally, especially in the beginning, a few Christian faculty members criticized me because I was not instructing Protestant students in their religious traditions. That there was not even a small number of students interested in such instruction did not matter to them. They also questioned and challenged my credentials as a Christian, even though I had been officially ordained within a mainstream Protestant denomination. Part of their attack was fueled by the complaints of a few evangelical and fundamentalist Christian students who found my being openly gay and Christian disturbing and contradictory.[22] By coincidence my book *Gay Theology Without Apology*, in which I examine and present my Christian identity, was published at the time and provided a timely response to this criticism; but my most important response was to continue to be a resource for evangelical students by reserving the chapel for their services, helping to fund their speakers and events, and finding and employing an intern from the nearby seminary who identified as evangelical. I also met with the professors and helped them to plan and sponsor their own Sunday evening service for faculty and students who needed to celebrate the Eucharist each week, a requirement for some but not all Protestants. Because my response was not to oppose and discourage the efforts of evangelical students, but to welcome and provide opportunities for them, I diffused what could have become a hostile environment. Although these students are not any more likely to agree with me, they are much less likely to attack and try to remove those who have different beliefs.

Developing Vespers has actually helped me to form and understand my own Christian identity and practice, even though I do not declare or put forth my own Christianity during services. Rarely do I say that as a Christian I do such-and-such. Saying so may be necessary at times, as I said in Chapter 5, when Christianity is misunderstood, ignored, or abused in a social context. Also, in pastoral counseling sessions I do talk with students about their and my Christianity when appropriate, and sometimes I am asked to speak or lead a discussion from a Christian perspective. I try to do the same with my gayness. I do advocate for gay issues when necessary, talk with students about their and my sexual/affectional identity in counseling sessions when appropriate, and give talks and serve on panels as a gay man when asked to. But in worship services I purposefully step back from my own identity because I do not want it to be a model that others copy or react to. Instead, I try to create an environment and provide a means that will enable them to develop their own identity. To succeed I must not let my own particular set of experiences limit and define who attends and what occurs at Vespers. I must effectively reach beyond myself to welcome whomever is searching for what is most meaningful to them.

Oddly enough, not continually declaring myself as a Christian allows me to feel more certain of my Christian identity. By not talking about myself as a Christian, I have come closest to understanding and doing the kind of work that Jesus Christ did. His work was about crossing social borders and building bridges across our personal differences; and he did his work without insisting that the people he reached out to become like him. One of the most influential biblical stories for me is the Gospel according to Matthew 8:5-13 and Luke 7:1-10. A Roman centurion—certainly an unpopular and despised figure in an occupied land—comes to Jesus and asks him to heal his paralyzed servant: "I am not worthy to have you come under my roof; but only say the word, and my servant will be healed." Jesus is so impressed by his sincerity that he says, "Not even in Israel have I found such faith" and "Go; be it done for you as you have believed." Jesus does not convert or change him, does not try to bring him into the fold. He simply recognizes the goodness within the man and helps him to see it for himself.[23] This story illustrates the kind of influence that I wish to have on students' spiritual development—to help them become more of themselves and not to become like me or what I may want them to be.

I know that many Christians oppose or cannot understand being a Christian without proclaiming it. For them, worship services provide the opportunity to talk about and declare their love for and loyalty to Jesus, and evangelizing means convincing non-believers of Jesus Christ's superiority. Simply to do good for others without saying that they are doing it for and because of Jesus makes no sense to them. But their preoccupation with talking about Jesus makes no sense to me. They are like a proud father who makes his friends listen to his never-ending boasting about his favorite son; and by doing so makes them less inclined to know and like the boy. I suppose the believers in any organized religion feel compelled to insist on the superiority of their deity, founder, prophet, or teacher; but such triumphalism, especially as I have seen it practiced in mainstream Protestantism, seems to impose and coerce rather than listen to and learn from others. If Jesus and his work have the power to heal and change people, we should not need an advertising campaign to prove it.

As a Christian, I have not moved into my own identity without some discomfort and hesitation—after all, talking about and praising Jesus is expected of Christian clergy. But I am not without access to a non-triumphalist Christian tradition, and one of the upholders of that tradition is Dietrich Bonhoeffer, the German theologian who was imprisoned and executed for his resistance to Nazi rule. I do not equate or compare my work to his, but I do find his view of Christian identity and practice helpful and applicable. Bonhoeffer's work was shaped by the tension and movement between prayer with a small group of committed Christians, on the one hand, and making common cause with non-Christians in the public arena on the other. The "prayer" part involved a low-profile, non-public, intense loyalty to Jesus Christ. The "action" part was not Christian-identified; and he spoke of "incognito Christians" connecting with all kinds people in the secular arena.[24]

Bonhoeffer's advice is especially helpful because I work at a secular university rather than in parish and am expected to make connections with the various divisions, departments, offices, and constituencies of the university. But my work has also led me to adjust and understand differently the "prayer" aspect of his advice. The group of students who come to Vespers have become for me what was "the small group of clearly committed Christians" for Bonhoeffer. Even though they may not be clearly committed Christians, they reflect more accurately the mixed, inclusive group of diverse people who gathered around Jesus than do most of today's Christian gatherings. But historical accuracy is not my reason for valuing the Vespers crowd as my religious community. I do so because they are the people with whom I most intensely pray and meditate and the people with whom I experience and share the deepest commitment and loyalty to spiritual honesty and growth.

As some may call my Christianity into question, so some also wonder about the focus of worship at Vespers.

SO, WHO OR WHAT IS WORSHIPED HERE?

After entering a church, temple, or mosque, one can usually discern without much difficulty who or what is worshiped. The architecture, seating, and interior design direct one to an altar, raised platform, or center. The ceremony names and glorifies a divine being, force, or presence. After entering Vespers for the first time, one may not be as certain about what or who is being worshiped. There is no altar or established liturgy. When I talk to students after they have visited for the first time, they tell me that their first impressions were as follows: They were surprised. Even though they heard that the service would not be "churchy," they still expected and were concerned that it would be more of "the same old thing." So, they were grateful for the informality and the ease with which they could sit among and talk with others or simply be quiet. After they were settled in, they did not feel that they would have to do anything that they did not want to do, but that they would be able to do something that meant something to themselves.

The physical space is not organized to recognize, name, and worship a particular God, but its design and use is intentional. Everyone and everything (except for those who choose to sit on the perimeter of benches) is on the same level; and the concentric seating gives people a view of each other. Visual attention is diffused rather than focused, voluntary rather than directed. The lighting is subdued and highlights no person or object. To be with others comfortably and privately is an initial and lasting impression. That which is worshiped—respected, honored, celebrated, and served—is the possibility of self-in-relation. People return to Vespers with the expectation that the meaning of both self and other may be renewed, that they may affirm and be affirmed by others. This mutuality of giving to and getting from others is at the heart of Vespers.

Although no one faith, deity, or religion is singled out above the others and many faiths, deities, and religions are honored, I would be disingenuous if I did not admit to designing Vespers from a particular theology. To close I shall diagram and describe what I consider to be the various theologies under which worship is organized in our society; and then I shall outline my own theology.[25] I use the term "theology" to mean one's view, understanding, and relationship with God.

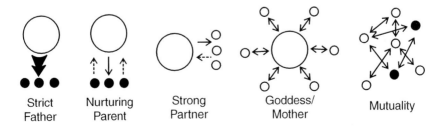

Strict Father   Nurturing Parent   Strong Partner   Goddess/ Mother   Mutuality

Probably the most common view of God is the fatherly figure who sits above the world and intervenes to help us when we are in need or to punish us when we are bad. In the diagram, in the first view, the big circle is God and the small circles are the people. As the arrow shows, the relationship with this God is one-way. God decides when, how, and where to intervene; and people listen for his orders. People are "children who should be seen and not heard;" and God is the Strict Father who knows what is best for them.

The second view of God is similar, but the Strict Father is replaced by the Nurturing Parent. Still removed from and an authority above the world, this God nonetheless listens to his children. They may question, argue with, and get angry at him; and God may change his mind in response to them. As the arrows show, this relationship is dialogical, but the arrow to God is dotted because God is still on top and all powerful.

The third view of God shifts to a horizontal relationship in which God is next to rather than above the people, a Strong—but more than equal—Partner. God walks beside, carries, and helps his people. The familiar story goes, "For a long time, I wondered where you were, God. I wanted you beside me, but when I looked behind me as I struggled through life I saw only one set of footprints. Then I realized that the footprints were yours and you had been carrying me."

The fourth view is the traditional Goddess in the middle of her children as an All-Giving Mother (different from Starhawk's Goddess-as-self quoted earlier). The Goddess nourishes and gives unconditionally much as a mother's breast feeds her children. They love their Goddess out of gratitude for life and love. She is often imaged as Earth Mother; and the ecology movement encourages and warns us to love and take care of our Mother because without her we die.

Personally, I have trouble with these four views of God because they seem to be about relinquishing and turning over responsibility to someone we create to take care of our problems. Bonhoeffer agreed. He said that people tend to turn to God and organized religion when their human resources fail to secure solutions. They look to God and religion to rescue them. When problems arise, a childish dependence on or anger with the Father takes place. Psychologically and morally mature people, on the other hand, regard themselves as accountable for their own answers to life's questions and problems. When they fail, they do not appeal to God and religion.

For Bonhoeffer, these kinds of God are turned to and experienced in people's weakness and resignation, not in their achievement and strength. They are not the kinds of God to whom people turn when they are self-confident, responsible, strong, and exercising their human powers in full consciousness of a common destiny. Bonhoeffer did not mean to minimize or ignore the effect of loneliness, despair, and other troubles in people's lives; but he refused to place the responsibility for fixing those problems on an external divine figure. He insisted that people must work with each other and with God to solve these problems and to become strong together.[26]

The attention paid to personal feelings and problems in Vespers is done to develop and build such self-confidence and strength. The rituals are meant to help people identify and address their own concerns and to listen to the concerns of others, to respect and honor the differences among them and to find and forge what they have in common. Hopefully, people leave Vespers not with the assurance that a divine being has taken care of their problems for them, but that they—in the company of others—have come to understand a little better how to deal with those problems. So, where is God in all of this interpersonal ritualizing? The theology or view of God underlying the design and work of Vespers is as follows:

In the fifth view of God, the diagram has no large circle to represent God. The small circles remain as people, and, if the diagram could show it, these circles would increase greatly in number and color, be represented in three-dimensional relationship to each other, and be connected by an array of different kinds of arrows. The people are given more attention and differentiation than in the other diagrams; and the arrows do not represent the relationship between people and God. Instead, the arrows are God.

I understand God not as above, outside, or in the center of us, but as among and between us. To describe my God is to describe what happens between us that makes us good, makes us more fully human, makes our lives ultimately meaningful. The connections among ourselves—the often awkward, difficult, challenging, satisfying, comforting, nurturing, thrilling demands that we put on and experience with one another—are God making us, creating us as fully human. In my theology, God is the mutuality in our relationships, the compelling and transforming power that brings together, reconciles, and creates us.

I believe that we are created and destroyed in our relationships. The creative power of mutuality—of God—can be found in our relationships when we learn from one another and act on our own and one another's behalf. As the writer James Baldwin said, "Our responsibility in this, our life, is to try to deal with each other and to work toward each other's freedom."[27] The destruction wrought by the absence of mutuality—when we ignore, subdue, and destroy one another—is evidenced by domestic violence, child abuse, terrorism, poverty, alienation, discrimination, and selfishness.

We come to know, believe in, and understand God as mutuality in the physical intimacy and exchanges of yes and no with our lovers, in our jobs when our contributions are valued and we value the contributions of others, or in any situation or relationship—social, sexual, political, economic—in which we take seriously and are taken seriously by others, need and depend on one another, initiate and follow, welcome and are welcomed, challenge and are challenged, encourage and are encouraged, take risks and find rest. God is "the loving of the other as you want to be loved" that creates a community in which the gifts and talents of all are welcome, developed, considered necessary, and recognized as special.

To worship God is to honor and respect one another, to affirm, criticize, and challenge one another, to give and receive within our relationships as if our lives depended on the exchange of human talents, to be available to and to seek out relationships beyond our own immediate experience, to change destructive relationships, to take advantage of and to nurture mutuality in our relationships, to use and expand the mutuality in our interpersonal relationships as a force and model for our society, our culture, and our relationships with the environment and planet, to build inclusive communities in which all—people, plants, and animals—are valued.

RETURNING FAVORS—
A NEW KIND OF LEADERSHIP ROLE

I believe that each of us is favored—or graced—with different talents and gifts that can be expressed or suppressed, that develop or wither, as we interact with others. This belief underlies and shapes my work. Such work is not all about making people feel good. It involves conflict and criticism, calling people to take responsibility, to use and develop their gifts. This work is not simply about uncovering and discovering our inner—perhaps hidden—true selves as much as it is about becoming and creating ourselves in various relationships with others.

I have changed quite a bit since I began as a college chaplain and professor. I feel as though I have become more of myself, and yet I am different and do my work differently than how I did it before. I have shifted away from performing for others to interacting with them. My job combines two vocations—professor and preacher—for which performance, authority, and independence have traditionally been distinguishing characteristics. I sometimes recall my instinctive aversion to that part of the ordination ceremony in which I was called to be "set apart" as a clergyman, because that instinct has since been affirmed many times as I have seen that effective and meaningful ministry is about being "set among" people and our personal and social messes. Over the years I have learned that my students are much less interested in being "wowed" by whatever brilliance and speaking abilities I may have than they are in talking with me about themselves. Impressing them is not what they want or need, nor is it what I want or need. They respond better and contribute more in informal settings and casual conversations than in lectures and church, and I have found that I do too. As I have lost interest in the conventional, distinguishing characteristics of my two professions, I have taken on others that I hope are reflected in my work and in this book: interacting, encouraging, and listening.

Ten years ago I probably would have considered these characteristics as too "hokey," sentimental, and nonintellectual and would have been too embarrassed to write about them. But as one of the theorists I cited in Chapter 2 claims, "Affect is the bedrock of cognition."[28] We learn better and are more curious when our experiences and feelings are taken seriously. More important, our survival and livelihood on this planet depend on our ability and willingness to build inclusive communities in which we interact across our differences and encourage and listen to one another. This is a lesson that I learned from the way my father responded to me, and it is the way I have used to become more fully human with others and to help them become more fully human with me.

Notes

Preface

1. See for example *The New York Times,* Kate Zernike, "Gay Couples Are Accepted As Role Models at Exeter," June 12, 2000, p. A20; "Gay Teacher's Disclosure Spurs Debate," June 11, 2000, section 1, p. 36; Katharine Q. Seelye, "Clinton Appoints Gay Man As Ambassador As Congress Is Away," June 5, 1999, p. A16; and Barbara Stewart, "The Pastor's Tale," October 1, 1995, section 2, p. 4.

2. Degrees of "selectivity" are used in college guide books to measure standards for admission at colleges and universities. See Edward T. Custard, John Katzman, Tom Meltzer, and Zachary Knower, *The Princeton Review Student Advantage Guide to the Best 310 Colleges,* 1997 Edition (New York: Random House, 1996).

Chapter 1

1. Tomie de Paola, *Oliver Button Is a Sissy* (San Diego: Harcourt Brace Jovanovich, 1979).

2. Alain Berliner, *Ma Vie en Rose* (Culver City, CA: Sony Pictures Entertainment, 1997).

3. Eve Kosofsky Sedgwick, "How to Bring Your Kids Up Gay," *Social Text* 29 (1991): 18-26; and *Epistemology of the Closet* (Berkeley: University of California Press, 1990), pp. 42-43.

4. Alan P. Bell, Martin S. Weinberg, and Sue Kiefer Hammersmith, *Sexual Preference: Its Development in Men and Women* (Bloomington: Indiana University Press, 1981). See also Richard C. Friedman, *Male Homosexuality: A Contemporary Psychoanalytic Perspective* (New Haven, CT: Yale University Press, 1988), pp. 33-48; and Richard Green, *The "Sissy Boy Syndrome" and the Development of Homosexuality* (New Haven, CT: Yale University Press, 1987), pp. 370-390.

5. See Friedman, *Male Homosexuality,* and Green, *The "Sissy Boy Syndrome."* For an overview of psychoanalytic approaches to male homosexuality, see Kenneth Lewes, *The Psychoanalytic Theory of Male Homosexuality* (New York: Simon and Schuster, 1988).

6. American Psychiatric Association, *Diagnostic and Statistical Manual of Mental Disorders,* Third Edition (DSM-III) (Washington, DC: American Psychiatric Association, 1980), pp. 264-266. See also Stephen F. Morin and Esther D. Rothblum, "Removing the Stigma: Fifteen Years of Progress," *American Psychologist,* 46 (1991): 947-949. An exception to the nearly silent response to the new diagnosis is Lawrence Mass, *Dialogues of the Sexual Revolution,* Volume 1, *Homosexuality and Sexuality* (Binghamton, NY: Harrington Park Press, 1990), p. 214.

7. Ibid. and DSM-IV (1994), pp. 532-538 passim.

8. See David Kirby, "The Second Generation," *The New York Times,* June 8, 1998, p. B7.

9. See Nina Bernstein, "Suit Alleges Frequent Abuse of Gay Children in Foster Care," *The New York Times,* January 16, 1999, pp. B1, B2; Katherine Whitlock, *Bridges of Respect: Creating Support for Lesbian and Gay Youth* (Philadelphia: American Friends Service Committee, 1988); William Celis III, "Schools Across the U.S. Cautiously Adding Lessons on Gay Life," *The New York Times,* January 6, 1993, p. A19; Rita Reed, *Growing Up Gay: The Sorrows and Joys of Gay and Lesbian Adolescence* (New York: W. W. Norton, 1997); Adam Mastoon, *The Shared Heart: Portraits and Stories Celebrating Lesbian, Gay, and Bisexual Young People* (New York: William Morrow, 1997); Lynette Holloway, "Young, Restless and Homeless on the Piers: Greenwich Village Reaches Out to Youths with Plan for Shelter and Services," *The New York Times,* July 18, 1998, pp. B1, B2; and David Lipsky, "To Be Young and Gay," *Rolling Stone,* August 6, 1998, pp. 55-64, 80, 82, 84-85.

10. See Randal C. Archibald, "A Gay Crusader Sees History on His Side," *The New York Times,* October 27, 1991, p. B2.

11. Sedgwick, "How to Bring Your Kids Up Gay," p. 18. See for example "Gay Teacher's Disclosure Spurs Debate," *The New York Times,* June 11, 2000, section 1, p. 36.

12. See "Schools' Books on Gay Families Stir Seattle," *The New York Times,* November 2, 1997, section 1, p. 24; Jonathan Mandell, "For Children with Gay Parents," *Newsday,* March 14, 1995, p. B2; Karen Freifeld and Myung Oak Kim, "Cardinal Virtue; Board Praised for Firing Fernandez," *Newsday,* February 15, 1993, City Edition, p. 3; Robert D. McFadden, "Bishop Assails School Leaders Over Lessons on Homosexuals," *The New York Times,* December 28, 1992, p. B8; Sasha Alyson, Fear of the Rainbow," *The New York Times,* December 30, 1992, p. A15; Liz Willen, "Gay Teachers Speak Out; Back New Curriculum in Queens," *Newsday,* September 25, 1992, p. 5.

13. Liz Willen, " 'Rainbow' Gone; Storm Not; New Teachers' Guide Doesn't Please Critics," *Newsday,* June 7, 1994, City Edition, p. A5; Liz Willen, "Joseph Fernandez Is Gone, But the Social Ills Remain; Fears and Loathing; Fernandez Ouster Leaves Gays Weary," *Newsday,* February 14, 1993, City Edition, p. 25; Peter Marks, "The Vote Against Fernandez; Fernandez Silently Sits in Real-Life People's Court," *The New York Times,* February 11, 1993, p. B12; Josh Barbanel, "Under 'Rainbow,' a War: When Politics, Morals and Learning Mix," *The New York Times,* December 27, 1992, section 1, p. 34; Nick Chiles and Liz Willen, "Beginning of the Rainbow; Guide's Path Strewn with Problems," *Newsday,* December 17, 1992, City Edition, p. 4.

14. As quoted and discussed by Joseph A. Fernandez, "Stop Smearing the Rainbow!," *Newsday,* November 11, 1992, City Edition, p. 54.

15. Steven Lee Myers, "How a 'Rainbow Curriculum' Turned into Fighting Words," *The New York Times,* December 13, 1992, section 4, p. 6. See Leslea Newman, *Heather Has Two Mommies* (Boston: Alyson, 1991) and Michael Willhoite, *Daddy's Roommate* (Boston: Alyson, 1991).

16. For a discussion on the essentialist/constructionist debate, see Diana Fuss, *Essentially Speaking: Feminism, Nature and Difference* (New York: Routledge, 1989) and Steven Epstein, "Gay Politics, Ethnic Identity: The Limits of Social Constructionism," *Socialist Review* 17 (May-August 1987): 9-54. For a collection of essays by constructionist theorists, see Diana Fuss, ed., *Inside/Out: Lesbian The-*

ories, Gay Theories (New York: Routledge, 1991). For evidence of inborn gayness in the natural sciences see Simon LeVay, *The Sexual Brain* (Cambridge, MA: MIT Press, 1993).

17. Sedgwick, *Epistemology of the Closet*, p. 43.

18. Judith Butler, *Gender Trouble: Feminism and the Subversion of Identity* (New York: Routledge, 1990), p. vii. See also Liz McMillen, "Judith Butler Revels in the Role of Troublemaker," *Chronicle of Higher Education*, May 23, 1997, pp. A14-A15.

19. Butler, *Gender Trouble*, p. xi.

20. As quoted in Sedgwick, "How to Bring Your Kids Up Gay," p. 18. See also Mike King, "Suicide Watch," *Advocate* (Los Angeles), November 12, 1996, pp. 41-44; and Gary Remafedi, ed., *Death by Denial: Studies of Suicide in Gay and Lesbian Teenagers* (Boston: Alyson, 1994).

21. Bernstein, "Suit Alleges Frequent Abuse of Gay Children in Foster Care," pp. B1, B2.

22. Donna J. Haraway, *Simians, Cyborgs, and Women: The Reinvention of Nature* (New York: Routledge, 1991), pp. 196, 199.

23. See Lev Raphael, *Journeys and Arrivals: On Being Gay and Jewish* (Boston: Faber and Faber, 1996); Reinaldo Arenas, *Before Night Falls*, trans. Dolores M. Koch (New York: Viking Penguin, 1993); Joseph Beam, ed., *In the Life: A Black Gay Anthology* (Boston: Alyson, 1986); Ann Heron, ed., *One Teenager in Ten: Testimony by Gay and Lesbian Youth* (Boston: Alyson, 1983; New York: Warner, 1986); Nancy Adair and Casey Adair, *Word Is Out: Stories of Some of Our Lives* (New York: Dell; San Francisco: Glide, 1978); David Kopay and Perry Deane Young, *The David Kopay Story: An Extraordinary Self-Revelation* (New York: Arbor House, 1977; Priam Books, 1980); and Howard Brown, *Familiar Faces, Hidden Lives: The Story of Homosexual Men in America Today* (New York: Harcourt Brace Jovanovich, 1976).

24. "The Boy in the Bubble," paper written for sociology course on Lesbian/bisexual/gay people in society, Wesleyan University, 1992.

25. "The Boy in the Bubble."

26. "The Pathologization of Proto-Gay Kids: Towards a Political Response," written for an independent tutorial on queer theory, Wesleyan University, 1992. See also Scott A. Hunt, "An Unspoken Tragedy: Suicide Among Gay and Lesbian Youth," *Christopher Street* 14/169 (1992): 28-30.

27. For the mythopoetic movement see Robert Bly and Bill Moyers, *A Gathering of Men* (New York: Public Affairs Television, 1990; Mystic Fire Video, 1991); Robert Bly, *Iron John: A Book About Men* (Reading, MA: Addison-Wesley, 1990); Robert Bly and Marion Woodman, *The Maiden King: The Reunion of Masculine and Feminine* (New York: Henry Holt, 1998); David B. Gilmore, *Manhood in the Making: Cultural Concepts of Masculinity* (New Haven, CT: Yale University Press, 1990); Robert Moore and Douglas Gillette, *King, Warrior, Magician, Lover: Rediscovering the Archetypes of the Mature Masculine* (New York: HarperCollins, 1990); Ray Raphael, *The Men from the Boys: Rites of Passage in Male America* (Lincoln: University of Nebraska Press, 1988); and Sam Keen, *To a Dancing God* (San Francisco: Harper & Row, 1970; 1990) and *Fire in the Belly: On Being a Man* (New York: Bantam, 1991). For the Million Man March see Garth Kasimu Baker-Fletcher, ed., *Black Religion and the Million Man March: Voices of the Future* (Maryknoll, NY: Orbis, 1998); Jeremiah A. Wright Jr., Colleen Birchett, and Frank Madison III, *When Black Men Stand Up for God: Reflections on the Million Man*

March (Chicago: African American Images, 1997). For the Promise Keepers see Dane S. Claussen, ed., *Standing on the Promises: The Promise Keepers and the Revival of Manhood* (Cleveland: Pilgrim, 1999); David G. Hackett, "Promise Keepers and Culture Wars," *Religion in the News*, June 1998, pp. 4-5, 18; and Thomas B. Edsall, "Movement Seeks to Revive Traditional Role for Men, *The Washington Post*, August 11, 1994, p. A11.

28. Garth Kasimu Baker-Fletcher, *Xodus: An African American Male Journey* (Minneapolis: Fortress, 1996); Michael Meade, *Men and the Water of Life: Initiation and the Tempering of Men* (San Francisco: HarperSanFrancisco, 1993); Michael S. Kimmel and Michael A. Messner, eds., *Men's Lives* (New York: Macmillan, Revised Edition,1992); Michael Messner, *Power at Play: Sports and the Problem of Masculinity* (Boston: Beacon, 1992); Stephen B. Boyd, *The Men We Long to Be: Beyond Lonely Warriors and Desperate Lovers* (New York: Macmillan, Second Edition, 1992); Richard Majors and Janet Mancini Billson, *Cool Pose: The Dilemmas of Black Manhood in America* (New York: Simon and Schuster, Touchstone, 1992); Keith Thompson, ed., *To Be a Man: In Search of the Deep Masculine* (Los Angeles: Jeremy P. Tarcher, 1991); and James B. Nelson, *The Intimate Connection: Male Sexuality, Masculine Spirituality* (Philadelphia: Westminster, 1988).

29. Ralph LaRossa, "Fatherhood and Social Change," in Kimmel and Messner, *Men's Lives*, pp. 521, 535. See also Patricia Cohen, "Daddy Dearest: Do You Really Matter?" *The New York Times*, July 11, 1998, pp. B7, B9; Ross D. Parke and Armin A. Brott, *Throwaway Dads: The Myths and Barriers That Keep Men from Being the Fathers They Want to Be* (Boston: Houghton Mifflin, 1999); Susan Faludi, *Backlash: The Undeclared War Against American Women* (New York: Doubleday, 1991), p. 65; W. Bradford Wilcox, "Conservative Protestant Childrearing: Authoritarian or Authoritative?," *American Sociological Review* 63/6 (December 1998): 796-809 and "Religion and Fatherhood: Exploring the Links between Religious Affiliation, Gender Role Attitudes, and Paternal Practices," Working Paper No. 13-97 (Department of Sociology, Princeton University, 1997).

30. Messner, *Power at Play*, pp. 7-8, 188-189 n. 1. Mircea Eliade, *Rites and Symbols of Initiation: The Mysteries of Birth and Rebirth*, trans. Willard R. Trask (New York: Harper Brothers, 1958; Revised Edition, Woodstock, CT: Spring Publications, 1993), p. 129, dispels the notion that puberty rites were or are universal to all tribal societies.

31. See Majors and Billson, *Cool Pose*, p. 51; and Jane Gross, "Male Bonding, But No Strippers: For Some, Stag Parties Yield to War Games and Ball Games," *The New York Times*, July 7, 1998, pp. B1, B8.

32. Hackett, "Promise Keepers and Culture Wars," pp. 4-5, 18.

33. Boyd, *The Men We Long to Be*, pp. 148-153, 163-168. For further defense of weekend retreats for men, see Meade, *Men and the Water of Life*, p. 10.

34. Boyd, *The Men We Long to Be*, p. 150.

35. Bly, *Iron John*, pp. 93-94.

36. Barry A. Kosmin and Seymour P. Lachman, *One Nation Under God: Religion in Contemporary American Society* (New York: Harmony, 1993), p. 232.

37. See Mihaly Csikszentmihalyi and Reed Larson, *Being Adolescent: Conflict and Growth in the Teenage Years* (New York: Basic, 1984), pp. 3-10, 260.

38. Alice Walker, *Anything We Love Can Be Saved: A Writer's Activism* (New York: Random House, 1997), p. 32.

39. Leo W. Simmons, ed., *Sun Chief: The Autobiography of a Hopi Indian* (New Haven: Yale University Press, 1942), as quoted by Jamake Highwater, *The Primal*

Mind: Vision and Reality in Indian America (New York: New American Library, Meridian Book, 1981), p. 176.

40. See Eliade, *Rites and Symbols of Initiation,* p. xii.

41. See Kimmel and Messner, *Men's Lives,* pp. 143-197; Messner, *Power at Play,* pp. 7-8; Majors and Billson, *Cool Pose,* p. 51; and Marvin M. Ellison, "Refusing to Be Good Soldiers: An Agenda for Men," in Susan E. Davies and Eleanor H. Haney, eds., *Redefining Sexual Ethics: A Sourcebook of Essays, Stories, and Poems* (Cleveland: Pilgrim, 1991), p. 191.

42. Ronald M. Green, *Religion and Moral Reason: A New Method for Comparative Study* (New York: Oxford University Press, 1988), pp. 136, see also 138-139, 143, 153, 160.

43. Tom F. Driver, *The Magic of Ritual: Our Need for Liberating Rites That Transform Our Lives and Our Communities* (San Francisco: HarperSanFrancisco, 1991), p. 102. For an example of what Driver sees as a "rationalization" for sacrificial origins, see Lionel Tiger, *Men in Groups* (New York: Random House, 1969).

44. To note that an antonym for "to perform" is "to fail" and for "absolute" is "mixed" or "imperfect" may be pushing the point too far, but the fear of failing to define an unmixed, perfect manhood would seem to undergird the desire to accomplish with certainty a perfect definition of manhood.

45. Some male writers in the 1970s challenged this preference for dominance and control. See Deborah S. David and Robert Brannon, eds., *The Forty-Nine Percent Majority: The Male Sex Role* (Reading, MA: Addison-Wesley, 1976); Joseph H. Pleck and Jack Sawyer, eds., *Men and Masculinity* (Englewood Cliffs, NJ: Prentice-Hall, Spectrum Book, 1974); Warren Farrell, *The Liberated Man: Beyond Masculinity—Freeing Men and Their Relationships with Women* (New York: Bantam, 1974); and Marc Feigen Fasteau, *The Male Machine* (New York: McGraw-Hill, 1974. The continuation of their approach into the 1980s and 1990s can be seen in the work of Baker-Fletcher, *Xodus;* Kimmel and Messner, *Men's Lives;* Majors and Billson, *Cool Pose;* Nelson, *The Intimate Connection;* and Boyd, *The Men We Long to Be.*

46. Bly and Moyers, *A Gathering of Men.*

47. E. M. Forster, *Maurice: A Novel* (New York: W. W. Norton, 1971), pp. 13-15.

48. Hermann Hesse, *Siddhartha,* trans. Hilda Rosner (New York: New Directions, 1951, 1957), p. 85.

49. Ibid., p. 86.

50. That baton-twirling is considered unusual behavior for boys is conveyed by these news stories: " 'True Showman' Takes Baton-Twirling Title," *Chronicle of Higher Education,* October 21, 1992, p. A44; and Susan Colwell, "Martin First Male on Baton Corps," *Ames High Web* (Ames, Iowa), September 28, 1984.

Chapter 2

1. Fritjof Capra, *The Turning Point: Science, Society, and the Rising Culture* (New York: Simon and Schuster, 1982; Bantam, 1983), p. 37. See also Ronald M. Green, *Religion and Moral Reason: A Method for Comparative Study* (New York: Oxford University Press, 1988), pp. 67-69; Lao-Tzu, *The Way of Life,* trans. Witter Bynner (New York: Capricorn, 1962), pp. 34-35; and John Heider, *The Tao of Leadership: Lao Tzu's "Tao Te Ching" Adapted for a New Age* (Atlanta: Humanics New Age, 1985).

2. John H. Westerhoff III, *Will Our Children Have Faith?* (New York: Seabury, 1976), p. 20.

3. Marc H. Ellis, *Toward a Jewish Theology of Liberation: The Uprising and the Future* (Maryknoll, NY: Orbis, 1987), p. 47.

4. Thich Nhat Hanh, *Peace Is Every Step: The Path of Mindfulness in Everyday Life* (New York: Bantam, 1991), pp. 68-69.

5. Ellis D. Evans, *Contemporary Influences in Early Childhood Education* (New York: Holt, Rinehart and Winston, 1971; Second Edition, 1975), pp. 41-43.

6. Thich Nhat Hanh, *Peace Is Every Step,* pp. 68-69.

7. Evans, *Contemporary Influences in Early Childhood Education,* pp. 255-286. See also John Dewey, *Experience and Education* (New York: Collier Macmillan, 1963).

8. See Evelyn Weber, *The Kindergarten: Its Encounter with Educational Thought in America* (New York: Teachers College Press, 1969), pp. 98-103.

9. Ibid., p. 100.

10. Ibid., pp. 127-135. See Patty Smith Hill and Grace Langdon, *Nursery School Procedures at Teachers College* (Geneva: Save the Children International Union, 1930); Agnes Burke, comp., *A Conduct Curriculum for the Kindergarten and First Grade: Directed by Patty Smith Hill* (New York: Scribner's Sons, 1924); and Patty Smith Hill, *Experimental Studies in Kindergarten Theory and Practice* (New York: Teachers College, Columbia University, 1915).

11. Jean Piaget, *The Moral Judgment of the Child* (1932), trans. Marjorie Gabain (New York: Free Press, 1965), p. 28; and Eleanor Duckworth (Interview with Jean Piaget), "Piaget Takes a Teacher's Look," *Learning,* October 1973, 25-27. See also Mary Ann Pulaski, *Understanding Piaget: An Introduction to Children's Cognitive Development* (New York: Harper & Row, 1980).

12. Duckworth, "Piaget Takes a Teacher's Look," p. 24.

13. Jerome S. Bruner, *Toward a Theory of Education* (Cambridge: Harvard University Press, 1961), p. 160.

14. Ibid.

15. Ibid., p. 161.

16. Ibid., p. 160.

17. Susan Isaacs, *Intellectual Growth in Young Children* (London: Routledge and Kegan Paul 1930), pp. 17-18, 102.

18. Ibid., pp. 37-38.

19. Ibid., p. 8.

20. Ibid., p. 35.

21. Ibid., pp. 57, 67, 97, 107.

22. Ibid., pp. 57, 64-65, 67, 80.

23. Susan Isaacs, *Social Development in Young Children* (New York: Routledge and Kegan Paul, 1933), pp. 3-5, 50, 64, 114, 122, 159, 163-164, 168, 237, 302-303, 352-362. For today's understanding and discussion of the origins of homosexuality, see Stephen F. Morin and Esther D. Rothblum, "Removing the Stigma: Fifteen Years of Progress," *American Psychologist,* 46 (1991): 947-949.

24. "Beginning Equal: The Project on Nonsexist Childrearing for Infants and Toddlers," *Equal Play: A Resource Magazine for Adults Who Are Guiding Young Children Beyond Stereotypes,* Summer-Fall 1982.

25. Charlotte Zolotow, with pictures by William Pene Du Bois, *William's Doll* (New York: Harper & Row, 1972; Harper Trophy, 1985).

26. See Beverly Slapin and Doris Seale, *Through Indian Eyes: The Native Experience in Books for Children* (Philadelphia: New Society, 1992); and Jon C. Stott, *Native Americans in Children's Literature* (Phoenix, AZ: Oryx, 1996).

Chapter 3

1. Paulo Freire, *Pedagogy of the Oppressed,* trans. Myra Bergman Ramos (1970; New York: Continuum, 1985; Revised Edition, 1993), pp. 52-67.

2. See my *Gay Theology Without Apology* (Cleveland: Pilgrim, 1993), pp. 105-126.

3. Hermann Hesse, *Siddhartha,* trans. Hilda Rosner (New York: New Directions, 1951, 1957).

4. Leslie Marmon Silko, *Ceremony* (New York: Viking Penguin, 1977; New American Library, 1978; Penguin Books, 1986).

5. Frantz Fanon, *Black Skin, White Masks,* trans. Charles Lam Markmann (New York: Grove, 1967).

6. Margaret Mead, *Male and Female: A Study of the Sexes in a Changing World* (New York: William Morrow, 1949), pp. 23, 129, 130, 132, 140.

7. Sigmund Freud, *An Outline of Psycho-Analysis,* trans. James Strachey (New York: W. W. Norton, 1929), p. 9.

8. Alfred C. Kinsey, Wardell B. Pomeroy, and Clyde E. Martin, *Sexual Behavior in the Human Male* (Philadelphia: W. B. Saunders, 1948), pp. 638, 650-651.

9. Aaron Fricke, *Reflections of a Rock Lobster: Growing Up Gay in America* (Boston: Alyson, 1982).

10. Terri Jewell, "Interview with Miss Ruth," in Makeda Silvera, ed., *Piece of My Heart: A Lesbian of Colour Anthology* (Toronto: Sister Vision, 1991), pp. 149-154; and Billy and Peaches Jones, "Growing Up with a Bisexual Dad," in Loraine Hutchins and Lani Kaahumanu, eds., *Bi Any Other Name: Bisexual People Speak Out* (Boston: Alyson, 1991), pp. 159-166.

11. Lyman A. Kellstedt, John C. Green, James L. Guth, and Corcoin E. Smidt, "Grasping the Essentials: The Social Embodiment of Religion and Political Behavior," in John C. Green et al., eds., *Religion and the Culture Wars* (Landam, MD: Rowman & Littlefield, 1996), pp. 174-192.

12. Pew Research Center for the People and the Press, *The Diminishing Divide . . . American Churches, American Politics* (Washington, DC: June 25, 1996), pp. 51, 52; Eric Stoltz, "Notes from a Community—Catholic and Gay," *America,* March 28, 1998, pp. 10-13; and in *The New York Times,* Gustav Niebuhr, "Politics: The Churches; Public Supports Political Voice for Churches," June 25, 1996, pp. A1, A18 and "Priest in a Liberal Parish Loses His Job for Breaking Church Rules," September 5, 1998, pp. B1, B7.

13. John J. McNeill, *The Church and the Homosexual* (Kansas City, MO: Sheed Andrews and McMeel, 1976).

14. John Boswell, *Christianity, Social Tolerance, and Homosexuality: Gay People in Western Europe from the Beginning of the Christian Era to the Fourteenth Century* (Chicago: University of Chicago Press, 1980).

15. Charles E. Curran, *Faithful Dissent* (Kansas City, MO: Sheed and Ward, 1986).

16. Barry A. Kosmin and Seymour P. Lachman, *One Nation Under God: Religion in Contemporary American Society* (New York: Harmony Books, 1993), pp. 10, 124, 200-203, 233, 270; National Conference of Catholic Bishops, *Always*

Our Children: A Pastoral Message to Parents of Homosexual Children and Suggestions for Pastoral Ministers; A Statement of the Bishops' Committee on Marriage and Family (Washington, DC: United States Catholic Conference, Inc., 1997).

17. See Edward T. Custard, John Katzman, Tom Meltzer, and Zachary Knower, *The Princeton Review Student Advantage Guide to the Best 310 Colleges,* 1997 ed. (New York: Random House, 1996), pp. 628-629.

18. Jane Tompkins, "Pedagogy of the Distressed," *College English* 52 (1990): 653- 660.

19. Martin S. Weinberg, Colin J. Williams, and Douglas W. Pryor, *Dual Attraction: Understanding Bisexuality* (New York: Oxford University Press, 1994).

20. Freud, *An Outline of Psycho-Analysis,* p. 9.

Chapter 4

1. Gary David Comstock, *Violence Against Lesbians and Gay Men* (New York: Columbia University Press, 1991), pp. 56-94. See also Evelyn Nieves, "Attacks on Gay Teen-Ager Prompt Outrage and Soul-Searching," *The New York Times,* February 19, 1999, p. A14.

2. Gloria Anzaldua, ed., *Making Face, Making Soul, Haciendo Caras: Creative and Critical Perspectives by Women of Color* (San Francisco: Aunt Lute Foundation, 1990), p. xv.

3. In addition to sources cited, the following are also relevant and important: Paula Gunn Allen, *The Sacred Hoop: Recovering the Feminine in American Indian Traditions* (Boston: Beacon, 1986); Beth Brant, ed., *A Gathering of Spirit: A Collection by North American Indian Women* (Ithaca, NY: Firebrand, 1988); Will Roscoe, ed., *Living the Spirit: A Gay American Indian Anthology* (New York: St. Martin's, 1988); Makeda Silvera, ed., *Piece of My Heart: A Lesbian of Colour Anthology* (Toronto: Sister Vision Press, 1991); Joanna Kadi, *Thinking Class: Sketches of a Cultural Worker* (Boston: South End, 1996); and Russell Leong, ed., *Asian American Sexualities: Dimensions of the Gay and Lesbian Experience* (New York: Routledge, 1996). See also Theresa Raffaele Jefferson, "Toward a Black Lesbian Jurisprudence," *Boston College Third World Law Journal,* Spring 1998, pp. 263-290.

4. Mary Catherine Bateson, *With a Daughter's Eye: A Memoir of Margaret Mead and Gregory Bateson* (New York: William Morrow, 1984).

5. Donna Haraway, *Simians, Cyborgs, and Women: The Reinvention of Nature* (New York: Routledge, 1991).

6. Audre Lorde, *Sister Outsider: Essays and Speeches* (Santa Cruz, CA: Crossing, 1984), p. 115. (All quotations from *Sister Outsider* reprinted with permission from *Sister Outsider* by Audre Lorde, copyright 1984. Published by the Crossing Press, Santa Cruz, California).

7. Ibid., p. 43.

8. Margaret Mead and James Baldwin, *A Rap on Race* (Philadelphia: Lippincott, 1971), p. 28.

9. Ibid., pp. 8-12.

10. Lorde, *Sister Outsider,* p. 114.

11. Audre Lorde, "There Is No Hierarchy of Oppressions," *Interracial Books for Children Bulletin* 14.3/4 (1983): 9.

12. Cherrie Moraga, *Loving in the War Years: Lo que nunca paso sus labios* (Boston: South End, 1983), p. 52. See also Gloria Anzaldua, "Speaking in Tongues:

A Letter to 3rd World Women Writers," in Cherrie Moraga and Gloria Anzaldua, eds., *This Bridge Called My Back: Writings by Radical Women of Color* (New York: Kitchen Table/ Women of Color, 1983), p. 171.

13. Barbara Smith, ed., *Home Girls: A Black Feminist Anthology* (New York: Kitchen Table/Women of Color, 1983), p. xxxii.

14. Lorde, *Sister Outsider,* p. 116.

15. Merle Woo, "Letter to Ma," in Moraga and Anzaldua, *This Bridge Called My Back,* p. 144. See also Merle Woo, "Our Common Enemy, Our Common Cause: Freedom Organizing in the Eighties," *Freedom Organizing Series #2* (Latham, NY: Kitchen Table/Women of Color, 1986), pp. 13-23.

16. Lorde, *Sister Outsider,* p. 116.

17. Smith, *Home Girls,* p. xxxii.

18. Moraga, *Loving in the War Years,* p. 53.

19. Woo, "Letter to Ma," p. 141.

20. Smith, *Home Girls,* p. xxxii.

21. Bateson, *With a Daughter's Eye,* pp. 102, 165.

22. Ibid., p. 94.

23. Ibid., pp. 27-28, 81, 27-28, 166.

24. Ibid., pp. 27, 85, 94, 166, 185.

25. Ibid., pp. 193-194.

26. Ibid., p. 191.

27. Ibid., p. 113.

28. Ibid., p. 191.

29. Ibid., pp. 165-166.

30. Anzaldua, "Speaking in Tongues," pp. 169, 170.

31. Ibid., p. 170.

32. Ibid.

33. Bateson, *With a Daughter's Eye,* pp. 139, 164, 166.

34. Ibid., p. 139.

35. Anzaldua, *Making Face,* p. xxv. See also Gloria T. Hull, "Researching Alice Dunbar-Nelson: A Personal and Literary Perspective," in Gloria T. Hull, Patricia Scott Bell, and Barbara Smith, eds., *All the Women Are White, All the Blacks Are Men, But Some of Us Are Brave: Black Women's Studies* (Old Westbury, NY: Feminist Press, 1982), p. 193; Virginia R. Harris and Trinity A. Ordona, "Developing Unity Among Women of Color: Crossing Barriers of Internalized Racism and Cross-Racial Hostility," in Anzaldua, *Making Face,* pp. 304-316; and Audre Lorde, *A Burst of Light* (Ithaca, NY: Firebrand, 1988), pp. 19-26.

36. Bateson, *With a Daughter's Eye,* pp. 110, 139-140.

37. Gloria Anzaldua, "La Prieta," in Moraga and Anzaldua, *This Bridge Called My Back,* p. 207.

38. Bateson, *With a Daugther's Eye,* p. 69.

39. Ibid., p. 196.

40. Ibid., p. 113, 191, 195-196.

41. Ibid., pp. 97, 120-121. Some current scholars of gender and sexuality, for example Jeffrey Weeks, *Sexuality and Its Discontents: Meanings, Myths, and Modern Sexualities* (London: Routledge & Kegan Paul, 1985), pp. 104-108, criticize Mead for not having been progressive enough. Weeks claims that even though she "rejects rigid sex dichotomization as wasteful," she "concludes *Male and Female* with a paean to the differences between, but complementary of, the sexes" and "advocates keeping the difference, but 'giving each sex its due.' " But Mead's stated pur-

pose in *Male and Female,* pp. 23, 129, 130, 132, 140, was "not to find out about the origins of our present ways of behaving" and she readily admitted that any "thinking about social origins" derived from her findings could only be "suggestive." Instead, she was concerned with how cross-cultural studies could "give us clues as to when and how certain behaviors are learned" in our own culture.

42. See Carol S. Robb, ed., in Beverly Wildung Harrison, *Making the Connections: Essays in Feminist Social Ethics* (Boston: Beacon, 1985), p. 1.

43. Haraway, *Simians, Cyborgs, and Women,* pp. 183-201.

44. Lorde, *Sister Outsider,* p. 58.

45. Haraway, *Simians, Cyborgs, and Women,* pp. 183-201. See also Robb, *Making the Connections,* p. xv, xix.

46. Haraway, *Simians, Cyborgs, and Women,* p. 191. She does, however, claim that the socially powerful are more likely to ignore knowledge that would threaten to change how and what they control, whereas the subjugated would seem to promise knowledge that could transform the world. The subjugated have the potential and advantage to spark inquiry that may unsettle preconceptions and familiar approaches.

47. Lorde, *Sister Outsider,* p. 59.

48. Haraway, *Simians, Cyborgs, and Women,* p. 191.

49. Bateson, *With a Daughter's Eye,* p. 119.

50. Ibid., p. 120.

51. Lorde, *Sister Outsider,* p. 115.

52. Mihaly Csikszentmihalyi, "The Pressured World of Adolescence," *Planned Parenthood Review,* Spring 1986, pp. 3-4. See also Mihaly Csikszentmihalyi and Reed Larson, *Being Adolescent: Conflict and Growth in the Adolescent Years* (New York: Basic, 1984), pp. 12, 15, 244, 251, 264-269. For a discussion of the socio-economic situation of adolescents, see Comstock, *Violence Against Lesbians and Gay Men,* pp. 102-109; Tina Rosenberg, "Helping Them Make It Through the Night," *The New York Times,* July 12, 1998, section 4, p. 16; and William Finnegan, *Cold New World: Growing Up in a Harder Country* (New York: Random House, 1998), pp. 1-92, and "Prosperous Times, Except for the Young," *The New York Times,* June 12, 1998, p. A21.

53. Paulo Freire, author of *Pedagogy of the Oppressed,* trans. Myra Bergman Ramos (1970; New York: Continuum, 1985; Revised Edition, 1993), pp. 26, 38-39, says that "an act is oppressive only when it prevents people from being more fully human" and that "dehumanization, which marks not only those whose humanity has been stolen, but also (though in a different way) those who have stolen it, is a *distortion* of the vocation of becoming more fully human."

54. Haraway, *Simians, Cyborgs, and Women,* p. 196.

55. Robert Davis, "Rights Issue Still Divided; Poll: Women More Tolerant, *USA Today,* April 26, 1993, pp. 1A, 10A.

56. See James B. Nelson, "Some Things You Have Taught a Straight, White Male During these 15 Years: Address at UCCL/GC's 15th Anniversary Dinner" (Athens, OH: United Church Coalition for Lesbian/Gay Concerns, 1987); J. Giles Milhaven, "How the Church Can Learn from Gay and Lesbian Experience" in Jeannine Gramick and Pat Furey, eds., *The Vatican and Homosexuality: Reactions to the "Letter to the Bishops of the Catholic Church on the Pastoral Care of Homosexual Persons"* (New York: Crossroad, 1988), pp. 216-223; E. Duane Wilkerson, "Struggling with Homophobia: What's at Stake for "Me?" *Open Hands: Resources for Ministries Affirming the Diversity of Human Sexuality,* Winter 1992, p. 12; R. A.

Rhoads, *Coming Out in College: The Struggle for a Queer Identity* (Westport, CT: Bergin & Garvey, 1994); and Wayne Schow, "Homosexuality, Mormon Doctrine, and Christianity: A Father's Perspective," in Ron Schow, Wayne Schow, and Marybeth Raynes, eds., *Peculiar People: Mormons and Same-Sex Orientation* (Salt Lake City: Signature, 1991), pp. 117-129.

Chapter 5

1. Herbert G. May and Bruce M. Metzger, eds., *The New Oxford Annotated Bible with the Apocrypha,* Revised Standard Version (New York: Oxford University Press, 1977), pp. 836-837.
2. *The New Oxford Annotated Bible with the Apocrypha,* p. 1375.
3. Ibid., pp. 1, 3.
4. Martin Buber, *I and Thou,* Second Edition, trans. Ronald Gregor Smith (New York: Charles Scribners, 1958), p. 29.
5. Thich Nhat Hanh, *Peace Is Every Step: The Path of Mindfulness in Everyday Life* (New York: Bantam, 1991), p. 9.
6. Van Morrison, "Wild Night," *The Best of Van Morrison* (New York: Polygram Records, 1990).
7. Published in *Open Hands: Resources for Ministries Affirming the Diversity of Human Sexuality,* Spring 1995, pp. 6-8.
8. The English word "radical" is derived from the Latin "radix," meaning "root."
9. The Book of Exodus. Quotes from *The New Oxford Annotated Bible,* pp. 3-4.
10. See Norman K. Gottwald, *The Hebrew Bible: A Socio-Literary Introduction* (Philadelphia: Fortress, 1985), pp. 211-213.
11. The Gospels according to Matthew 16:13-20; Mark 8:27-30; and Luke 9:18-22.
12. Starhawk, *The Spiral Dance: A Rebirth of the Ancient Religion of the Great Goddess* (San Francisco: Harper & Row, 1979), p. 89.
13. Starhawk, *Dreaming the Dark: Magic, Sex and Politics* (Boston: Beacon, 1982), p. 73.
14. *To High School and College Students: About the Book of Genesis,* Studies in Understanding the Bible Series (Charlotte, NC: United Ministries In Higher Education, 1994).
15. Donna Haraway, *Simians, Cyborgs, and Women: The Reinvention of Nature* (New York: Routledge, 1991) pp. 183-201. See also Carol S. Robb, ed., in Beverly Wildung Harrison, *Making the Connections: Essays in Feminist Social Ethics* (Boston: Beacon, 1985), p. xv, xix.

Chapter 6

1. Tom Driver, *The Magic of Ritual: Our Need for Liberating Rites That Transform Our Lives and Our Communities* (San Francisco: HarperCollins, 1992), pp. 52-75.
2. Driver, *The Magic of Ritual,* p. 238.
3. Paul Tillich, *Dynamics of Faith* (New York: Harper & Brothers, 1957; Harper Torchbook, 1958), pp. 1-4.
4. Thich Nhat Hanh, *Peace Is Every Step: The Path of Mindfulness in Everyday Life* (New York: Bantam, 1991), pp. 18-19.

5. My translation and adaptation of Genesis 2:7. See also Phyllis Trible, *God and the Rhetoric of Sexuality* (Philadelphia: Fortress, 1978), pp. 75-81.

6. My translation and adaptation of Genesis 1:27. See also Trible, *God and the Rhetoric of Sexuality,* pp. 12-21.

7. Leslie Marmon Silko, *Ceremony* (New York: Viking Penguin, 1977; New American Library, 1978; Penguin, 1986), p. 1.

8. My translation and adaptation of Exodus 3:13-14.

9. My translation and adaptation of Micah 6:8.

10. My translation and adaptation of Matthew 25:35-40.

11. James (Jimmy) E. Jones, "Why I Am a Muslim," in Edith S. Engel and Henry W. Engel, eds., *One God: Peoples of the Book* (New York: Pilgrim, 1990), pp. 120-124.

12. Hermann Hesse, *Siddhartha,* trans. Hilda Rosner (New York: New Directions, 1951), p. 113.

13. Paula Gunn Allen, *The Sacred Hoop: Recovering the Feminine in American Indian Traditions* (Boston: Beacon, 1986), pp. 13-14.

14. Alice Walker, *The Color Purple* (New York: Simon and Schuster; 1982; Pocket Books, 1982), pp. 202-203.

15. Audre Lorde, *Sister Outsider: Essays and Speeches* (Santa Cruz, CA: Crossing, 1984), pp. 36-37.

16. James B. Nelson, *The Intimate Connection: Male Sexuality, Masculine Spirituality* (Philadelphia: Westminster, 1988), p. 110-111.

17. Carter Heyward, *Touching Our Strength: The Erotic as Power and the Love of God* (San Francisco: Harper & Row, 1989), p. 131.

18. Starhawk, *Dreaming the Dark: Magic, Sex, and Politics* (Boston: Beacon, 1982), p. 11.

19. Heyward, *Touching Our Strength,* p. 73.

20. Starhawk, *The Spiral Dance: A Rebirth of the Ancient Religion of the Great Goddess* (San Francisco: Harper & Row, 1979), p. 105.

21. Herbert G. May and Bruce M. Metzger, eds., *The New Oxford Annotated Bible with the Apocrypha,* Revised Standard Version (New York: Oxford University Press, 1977), p. 816.

22. Tav Nyong'o, "Jesus, Wesleyan, and the Problem of Tolerance," *Hermes* (Wesleyan University), November 1993, pp. 11-14.

23. Jesus also distinguishes and honors outsiders as examples of great faith in the story of the good Samaritan (Luke 10:29-37) and the Syrophoenician woman (Matthew 15:21-28; Mark 7:24-30).

24. Here I rely on Larry Rasmussen, with Renate Bethge, *Dietrich Bonhoeffer—His Significance for North Americans* (Minneapolis: Fortress, 1990), pp. 57-70. See also Dietrich Bonhoeffer, "Thoughts on the Day of the Baptism of Dietrich Wilhelm Rudiger Bethge," *Letters and Papers from Prison,* ed. Eberhard Bethge, trans. Reginald H. Fuller et al. (London: SCM, 1953; New York: Macmillan 1972; New York: Simon and Schuster, Touchstone, enlarged ed., 1997), pp. 294-300.

25. See Isabel Carter Heyward, *The Redemption of God: A Theology of Mutual Relation* (Washington, DC: University Press of America, 1982); George Lakoff, *Moral Politics: What Conservatives Know that Liberals Don't* (Chicago: University of Chicago Press, 1996); and Gary David Comstock, *Gay Theology Without Apology* (Cleveland: Pilgrim, 1933), pp. 127-129.

26. Rasmussen, *Dietrich Bonhoeffer,* pp. 57-70.

27. Jere Real, "James Baldwin: A Rare Interview with a Legendary Writer," *Advocate* (Los Angeles), May 27, 1986, pp. 42-46.

28. Susan Isaacs, *Intellectual Growth in Young Children* (London: Routledge and Kegan Paul, 1930), pp. 17-18, 102.

Index

Order Your Own Copy of
This Important Book for Your Personal Library!

THE WORK OF A GAY COLLEGE CHAPLAIN
Becoming Ourselves in the Company of Others

_____ in hardbound at $39.95 (ISBN: 1-56023-360-5)

_____ in softbound at $19.95 (ISBN: 1-56023-361-3)

COST OF BOOKS_____

OUTSIDE USA/CANADA/
MEXICO: ADD 20%_____

POSTAGE & HANDLING_____
(US: $4.00 for first book & $1.50
for each additional book)
Outside US: $5.00 for first book
& $2.00 for each additional book)

SUBTOTAL_____

in Canada: add 7% GST_____

STATE TAX_____
(NY, OH & MIN residents, please
add appropriate local sales tax)

FINAL TOTAL_____
(If paying in Canadian funds,
convert using the current
exchange rate, UNESCO
coupons welcome.)

☐ **BILL ME LATER:** ($5 service charge will be added)
(Bill-me option is good on US/Canada/Mexico orders only;
not good to jobbers, wholesalers, or subscription agencies.)

☐ Check here if billing address is different from
shipping address and attach purchase order and
billing address information.

Signature_____

☐ **PAYMENT ENCLOSED: $**_____

☐ **PLEASE CHARGE TO MY CREDIT CARD.**

☐ Visa ☐ MasterCard ☐ AmEx ☐ Discover
☐ Diner's Club ☐ Eurocard ☐ JCB

Account # _____

Exp. Date_____

Signature_____

Prices in US dollars and subject to change without notice.

NAME_____

INSTITUTION_____

ADDRESS_____

CITY_____

STATE/ZIP_____

COUNTRY_____ COUNTY (NY residents only)_____

TEL_____ FAX_____

E-MAIL_____

May we use your e-mail address for confirmations and other types of information? ☐ Yes ☐ No
We appreciate receiving your e-mail address and fax number. Haworth would like to e-mail or fax special
discount offers to you, as a preferred customer. **We will never share, rent, or exchange your e-mail address
or fax number.** We regard such actions as an invasion of your privacy.

Order From Your Local Bookstore or Directly From
The Haworth Press, Inc.
10 Alice Street, Binghamton, New York 13904-1580 • USA
TELEPHONE: 1-800-HAWORTH (1-800-429-6784) / Outside US/Canada: (607) 722-5857
FAX: 1-800-895-0582 / Outside US/Canada: (607) 722-6362
E-mail: getinfo@haworthpressinc.com
PLEASE PHOTOCOPY THIS FORM FOR YOUR PERSONAL USE.
www.HaworthPress.com

BOF00